MARTIN LUTHER
MASTER OF DECEIT

1483-1546

DR. MAX D. YOUNCE

MARTIN LUTHER
MASTER OF DECEIT
DR. MAX D. YOUNCE

Unless otherwise indicated, all Scripture quotations are taken from the King James Translation of the Bible.

Library of Congress
Control Number: 2008901289

ISBN-13: 978-0-9815225-0-0

First Printing 2008

FOR INFORMATION CONTACT:
Dr. Max D. Younce
P.O. Box 573
Walnut Grove, MN 56180

Or, please visit our web site at www.heritagebbc.com
Online ordering is available for all products.

Printed in the USA
by Morris Publishing
3212 East Highway 30
Kearney, NE 68847
800-650-7888

"That we henceforth be no more children, tossed to and fro, and carried about with every wind of doctrine, by the sleight of men, and cunning craftiness, whereby they lie in wait to deceive;"

The Bible, Ephesians 4:14

Oh what a tangled web we weave,
When first we practice to deceive!

Sir Walter Scot

DEDICATION

This book is dedicated to the person who, with a desire to know the truth, will compare what I have written in these pages to the Bible, and take to heart the statements that are found in this book.

More than that, I pray that the person who reads these pages will understand that eternal life is not found in a ritual, or a church; but, in a person. It is found in our Wonderful Savior, the Lord Jesus Christ, Who said,

> *"I am the way, the truth, and the life: no man cometh unto the Father, but by me."* (John 14:6).

Even more, I pray that the person who reads this book will have the courage to say, "I am tired of being deceived by a man who has been dead for 460 years. I believe that Jesus Christ died for me, period! Christ's last words on the cross were, "*It is finished...,*" and because of that only, I know I have eternal life!"

> *"For God so loved the world, that he gave his only begotten Son, that whosoever believeth in him should not perish, but have everlasting life.* (John 3:16)"

> *"These things have I written unto you that believe on the name of the Son of God; that ye may know that ye have eternal life, and that ye may believe on the name of the Son of God."* (I John 5:13).

ACKNOWLEDGMENTS

I want to thank our faithful Sunday Night Congregation for their listening patience as I read and taught them each and every chapter of this book. When I asked them if they were getting bored, or thought the teaching was too strong; their comment was, "Give it to them, Pastor! They need to know!"

I am deeply grateful to those Christians who have financially given to make the publication of this book possible. It is wonderful to see the love they have for those who Luther has so deceived, evidenced by their giving. Without them, this book would not be in print.

"So then faith cometh by hearing, and hearing by the word of God." (Romans 10:17).

TABLE OF CONTENTS

FOREWORD

Or, An Answer To The Critics

I have been criticized for giving the credit to Martin Luther for the statement on Page 174, Par. C. of *Luther's Small Catechism*, where he states "...because infants, too, *can believe.*" My critic responded, "Martin Luther did not say that. That is only in the *explanation* of the Catechism."

I submit to you that Martin Luther *did* say that and he most assuredly *believed* that. He takes up the subject of Infant Baptism in his **Large Catechism on Page 86**, of my copy; **and** on **Page 87, Par. 52**, he states, "Further, we are not primarily concerned whether the baptized person believes or not, for in the latter case Baptism does not become invalid." In Par. 53, he states, "...Baptism is valid, even though faith be lacking. He nails it down in Par. 55 when he concludes,

> **"As we said, even if infants did not believe; which, however is *not* the case, as we have proved-still their Baptism would be valid and no one should rebaptize them."**

Thank you, Mr. Luther!

I have two Catechisms from the Missouri Lutheran Synod. One says, *Luther's Small Catechism* on the front; ***but,*** on the inside title page we find it states, "A Short Explanation of Dr. Martin Luther's Small Catechism, A Handbook of Christian Doctrine." Then, the next page says, "Dr. Martin Luther's Small Catechism." Well now! Which is it? Is it the Catechism; or an explanation by someone else; or the two mixed together? How confusing! I have found from my investigation that the latter (the two mixed together) is the case. The Small Catechism has been expanded with quotations and statements from the Large Catechism and Martin Luther's many other writings. Certainly it would be more helpful to the Lutheran student if these additions had been duly noted. In fact, Martin Luther encouraged this. Here are his words from the Preface to the Small Catechism, Eighth Paragraph.

> **"Thirdly, after you have thus taught them this Short Catechism, then take up the Large Catechism, and give them also a richer and fuller knowledge. Here explain at large every commandment, [article,] petition, and part with its various works, uses, benefits, dangers, and injuries, as you find these abundantly stated in many books written about these matters."** (I am sure these "many books" would be works of Martin Luther).
>
> (http://www.edccs.com/redeemer/beliefs/small-catechism.htm#preface).

Yes, the statement "...because infants, too, *can believe*" did come from Martin Luther and is exactly what he believed!

Another thing I have routinely been scolded for is saying that Martin Luther was not a saved man. I have been accused of standing in the place of God, Himself, because I say that Martin Luther was not a saved man.

God's Word is very clear about this. We are to judge the Gospel message. Our very salvation depends upon it!

> *"Beloved, believe not every spirit, but try the spirits whether they are of God: because many false prophets are gone out into the world."* (I John 4:1).

> *"Now I beseech you, brethren, mark them which cause divisions and offences contrary to the doctrine which ye have learned; and avoid them.* (V.17).

> *For they that are such serve not our Lord Jesus Christ, but their own belly; and by good words and fair speeches deceive the hearts of the simple."* (Romans 16:17-18).

One web author, who writes about Martin Luther, very aptly commented, "If these beliefs (meaning those of Martin Luther) were presented you anonymously, would you not say the author was a heretic, without saving faith in the Lord Jesus Christ? Strange, then, that with Luther's name attached, excuses are made, such as: "You misunderstand what he says"; Something was lost in the translation"; "The words don't have the same meaning they had in the 16th Century..."

(www.rapidnet.com~jbeard/exposes/luther.general.htm).

Approximately 16 years after Luther had written his Catechisms, he died. If at any time in his last 16 years of life he had changed his mind concerning his beliefs, it would have flashed over Europe like a forest fire!

In those times when all his friends were listening to his so-called "Divine Discourses" and supposedly writing down every word that fell from his lips, could he not have said, "Away with the Catechisms!" "Away with the Sacraments!" "Away with Baptism!"? If he had done so, the course of History would have been changed in a big way! The ***true*** Gospel of our Lord Jesus Christ would have spread over Europe like a flood.

But did he? We all know that he did NOT change his mind about ANY of his teachings. Instead, the religion of works that Martin Luther taught in ALL his writings, ALL of his life were exported all over the world. Martin Luther believed that you have to be baptized to be saved. He said it over and over again. Here are his words from Page 174 of *The Small Catechism.*

> **"II. THE BLESSINGS OF BAPTISM. What does Baptism give or profit? It works forgiveness of sins, delivers from death and the devil, and gives eternal salvation to all who believe this, as the words and promises of God declare."**

Or, from his *Large Catechism*, P. 83, #24.

> **"To put it most simply, the power, effect, benefit, fruit, and purpose of Baptism IS TO SAVE."**

Nor did Luther believe that you had to have faith for baptism to be valid.

> **"Further, we are not primarily concerned whether the baptized person believes or not, for in the latter case, Baptism does NOT become invalid."** (*Large Catechism*, P. 87, Par. 52).

> **"Baptism is valid, even though FAITH be lacking."** (Par. 53).

Do these sound like the words of a saved man? Absolutely not!

> *"For by grace are ye saved through faith; and that not of yourselves: it is the gift of God: Not of works, lest any man should boast."*
>
> (Ephesians 2:8-9).

> *"He that believeth on the Son hath everlasting life: and he that believeth not the Son shall not see life; but the wrath of God abideth on him."*
>
> (John 3:36).

The Bible teaches that the fruit of the believer is another believer. Matthew 7:15-20 explains this very clearly.

> *"BEWARE OF FALSE PROPHETS, which come to you in sheep's clothing, but inwardly they are ravening wolves.*(V.15).

> *Ye shall know them by their fruits. Do men gather grapes of thorns, or figs of thistles?*(V.16*)*.
>
> *Even so every good tree bringeth forth good fruit; but a corrupt tree bringeth forth evil fruit.*(V.17).
>
> *A good tree cannot bring forth evil fruit, neither can a corrupt tree bring forth good fruit.* (V.18).
>
> *Every tree that bringeth not forth good fruit is hewn down, and cast into the fire.* (V.19).
>
> *Wherefore by their fruits ye shall know them."* (V.20).
>
> (Matthew 7:15-20).

Our Lord is teaching a lesson in this Scripture passage about "*false prophets*." The "*trees*" picture the prophet's message and the "*good fruit*" is a born-again Christian, and the "*evil fruit*" is an unbeliever.

What kind of "*fruit*" did Martin Luther's teachings bear? "*Evil fruit*" from a "*corrupt tree*." The fruit of Martin Luther's corrupt message is his followers who have been convinced by his puppet preachers that their baptism as projected in his Catechisms, will gain them entry into Heaven. They are *so* deceived and Hell will be their reward, if they believe his philosophy.

> *"...Depart from me, ye cursed, into everlasting fire, prepared for the devil and his angels:"*
>
> (Matthew 25:41).

> *"Beware of false prophets, which come to you in sheep's clothing, but inwardly they are ravening wolves."*
>
> (Matthew 7:10).

This is a perfect description of Martin Luther, the Master of Deceit! I will say it again! Martin Luther was never a saved man, as evidenced by his own writings.

Introduction

Why Did I Write This Book?

My first reason would be that I believe it is why the Lord brought me to this area to begin with. I needed to learn about the effects of the false cults of Lutheranism and Catholicism first hand. I am not ashamed to say these organizations are cults; as they are not Scriptural in the tenets they teach! In their appearance to the world, they are just like the other cults.

I call this the "iceberg effect." We all know that when we see an iceberg, we must give it a wide berth, because only about 1/8 of its volume appears above the water. The part that sank the great Titanic was the 7/8 below the waterline. Christians who are serious about witnessing need to know about the 7/8 of Lutheran doctrine which lurk just below the surface and make shipwreck of hapless souls!

Of course, another important reason for coming here was the fact that this area needed an independent, fundamental church which preaches the *clear* Gospel of Jesus Christ.

Reason Number Two: If I had not come here I would still have been witnessing to those of all Lutheran denominations, making the same error that other Christians have in the past. That is: when a Lutheran (or Catholic) tells you, "I believe that Christ died to pay for my sins;" we are assuming those words mean the same thing to them as they do to me. Nothing could be further from the truth!

To me, believing that Jesus Christ died on the cross to pay for my sins, is the foundation of my Salvation. That is the basis for God accepting me into His Perfect Heaven. God sees my sin through the blood of His Dear Son, and accounts to me His perfect righteousness for that reason. This is my Scriptural basis for knowing I have eternal life,

> *"For he hath made him to be sin for us, who knew no sin; that we might be made the righteousness of God in him."* (II Corinthians 5:21).

Reason Number Three: It really bothers me to see the trend of many respected preachers and noted scholars of our day who recommend the sermons of Luther; or make comments about Luther such as "He wasn't going to move from salvation by faith (*sola fide*), salvation by grace (*sola gratia*) and salvation only by the Scripture (*sola scriptura*)." As we prove in the following pages of this book, Martin Luther simply just did not believe these things, and I hope that this book will help preachers become aware of this.

I have quoted below a paragraph from a fine article entitled "Martin Luther's Sacramental Gospel," which I found on the internet. This helps to validate my findings about Martin Luther and reveals there are others who have also become aware of this trend.

"Luther is quoted favorably by just about everyone in professing Christianity. Evangelicals and Fundamentalists often refer to him as a champion of "Justification By Faith ALONE." However, that is only half the story. It is absolutely amazing that very few seem to realize that Luther in fact believed that we are saved by "**faith alone through**

baptism." However, you can't have it both ways at the same time, "Faith Alone" and "Faith through Baptism." The **addition** of "through baptism" in effect **contradicts** "faith alone."

(www.rapidnet.com/~jbeard/bdm/luther/general.htm.)

Reason Number Four: Wrong assumptions about what Martin Luther taught about salvation; or what Lutheranism today teaches about how to be saved, can have drastic consequences in the life of a Christian. It can result in the "unequal yoke" of a saved person being married to an unsaved person.

> *"Be ye not unequally yoked together with unbelievers: for what fellowship hath righteousness with unrighteousness? and what communion hath light with darkness?"* (II Corinthians 6:14).

Many a bride or groom, years on down the line after the children arrive, have realized they are married to a lost person. How can this happen? It happens because the officiating pastor took the unsaved Lutheran person's statement "I believe that Jesus Christ died for the sins of the world; or, "My salvation is based on faith alone, and there are no works involved!" as proof that the person's faith is in Christ's finished work, alone, for salvation! They are unaware that Martin Luther teaches in his Catechisms that baptism is <u>not</u> a work. This is one of his most insidious, devilish, and damnable teachings. Here are his words.

> ***"Baptism is not a work which we do*** **but is a treasure which God gives and faith grasps,**

> **just as the *Lord Christ upon the cross is not a work*, but a treasure comprehended and offered to us in the word and received by faith**." (*Large Catechism*, Page 85, Par. #37).

This causes a great deal of unhappiness in families and sometimes results in the born-again Christian "caving in" to the wishes of their spouse and "the family." The family is insistent that the children should be baptized, and now enters the damnable doctrine of Infant Baptism with all its ludicrous paraphernalia.

In the words of one Lutheran pastor, "...Use plenty of water. Splash it around! Get the baptismal party a little wet. Let the children standing close by feel the water and hear the water in the baptism." (*Baptized: Marked for Living!,* John D. Hopper)

After all, Luther says the baptismal water is "Divine Water." (Large Catechism, Page 82, Par. #14). Martin Luther teaches that babies can believe! (*Small Catechism*, Pg.174, Par.C). During the ceremony, the God-parents answer for the children, "Yes, we believe," and it is said the Holy Spirit enters the child. Dare I say it? What hogwash!

A Lutheran, following the teachings of Martin Luther, believes that Christ only purchased our salvation when He died on the cross. All Lutherans, of all the different conferences that I am aware of, are drilled from childhood in Martin Luther's *Small Catechism*. They most emphatically believe that salvation can only be accomplished by the baptismal waters of what has been presented to them as "Holy Baptism;" as well as many other unscriptural teachings which Luther has propagated in his *Large* and *Small Catechisms*. Almost every Lutheran family has at least one *Small Catechism*. Hardly any families that I know of possess a *Large Catechism*; but, they would be found in almost every Lutheran pastor's library.

Here are Luther's words in his *Large Catechism*, P. 83, #24.

> **"To put it most simply, the power, effect, benefit, fruit, and purpose of Baptism IS TO SAVE."**

Furthermore, Martin Luther teaches that you do not even have to *have any faith* when you are baptized; therefore paving the way for infant baptism. Let me allow Luther to speak for himself.

> **"Further, we are not primarily concerned whether the baptized person believes or not, for in the latter case, Baptism does NOT become invalid."** (*Large Catechism*, P. 87, Par. 52).

> **"Baptism is valid, even though FAITH be lacking."** (Par. 53).

Even then, salvation for those following the teachings of Martin Luther is not a "done deal," as they say. According to Martin Luther, without the two Sacraments (i.e. Baptism and the Lord's Supper), no one can be a Christian. (*Large Catechism*, P.80). Luther states in his *Small Catechism*, P.169, Par. 243 that,

> **"There are only two such Sacraments, Holy Baptism and the Lord's Supper."**

In Paragraph 242 of Page 169, Luther says that,

> **"By a sacrament we mean a sacred act. – A. Instituted *by God Himself*; B. In which there are *certain visible means connected with His word*; and C. By which God offers, gives, and seals unto us THE FORGIVENESS OF SINS which Christ has earned for us."**

Now, in Luther's *Large Catechism*, Page 80, under "Baptism, Paragraph 1," he states that,

> **"...because without these (i.e. Baptism and the Lord's Supper) no one can be a Christian."**

Reason Number Five: Another false teaching of Martin Luther is that Lutheran pastors can forgive sins, using the same doctrine as the Catholic organization. Since Martin Luther agreed with the Roman Catholic organization that priests could be "mediators between God and man," and could forgive sin, he continued to propagate this false doctrine in his Catechisms. The Pope was able to get Martin Luther out of the Catholic Church; but, not even God, Himself, could get the Catholic Church out of Luther!

Luther's own words, as stated in his *Small Catechism*, P.188, under:

"CONFESSION AND ABSOLUTION.

What is Confession? **Confession embraces two parts. One is that we confess our sins; the other, that we received absolution, or forgiveness, from the pastor as from God Himself, and in nowise doubt, but firmly believe, that by it our sins are forgiven before God in Heaven."**

"How should we regard the absolution, or forgiveness of sins, pronounced by the Pastor?

We should regard the absolution as if pronounced by *God Himself,* and in no wise doubt, but *firmly believe,* that by it *our sins are forgiven before God in Heaven."*

Now Martin Luther has his followers brainwashed into believing that he and his preachers are standing in God's shoes, with the power to forgive your sins.

What more can one man do to stand in the way of God's Salvation than to teach that baptism saves; and that the Lord's Supper and the minister's forgiving of your sins will keep you saved? All this from a man who claims to believe the Scripture.

> *"For there is one God, and one mediator between God and men, the man Christ Jesus;"* (1 Timothy 2:5).

What more could he do? Much more! Martin Luther was a "master at deception." He presented his teachings in a very deceptive way. He took verses out of context, quoted only parts of verses; or, quoted verses and said they meant something else. He added to Scripture. He raised his Catechisms above the Word of God. In spite of, "sola fide, sola gratia, sola scriptura," it has always been, "The Gospel according to Martin Luther," not, the Gospel of our Lord Jesus Christ!

> *"Moreover, brethren, I declare unto you the gospel which I preached unto you, which also ye have received, and wherein ye stand;* (V.1).
>
> *By which also ye are saved, if ye keep in memory what I preached unto you, unless ye have believed in vain.* (V.1).
>
> *For I delivered unto you first of all that which I also received, how that Christ died for our sins according to the scriptures;* (V.3).
>
> *And that he was buried, and that he rose again the third day according to the scriptures:"* (V.4).
>
> (I Corinthians 15:1-4).

This book was not written as a history of Martin Luther's life, I leave that to others. As I have said, I have only "touched the tip of the iceberg" of Luther's false doctrine. All of this I have documented in the following pages.

Some have taken issue with the tone of my words, saying they are too harsh. To these folk I recommend a serious reading of Martin Luther's *"On the Jews and Their Lies;"* or his infamous pamphlet, *"Against the Murderous and Rapacious Hordes of the Peasants."* I write the way I do to attract people's attention! Which is just how Martin Luther wrote in his day. The response has indicated that it works. At least you can not accuse me of writing something that is inflammatory; or, that is used as an excuse to send 6 million Jewish souls into eternity! Hitler loved Luther and spread his writings filled with hatred for the Jewish people all through Germany

I also highly recommend that you take your Bible and read the whole of Matthew, Chapter 23. Pay particular attention to the words our precious Lord Jesus Christ used to talk to and about the Scribes and Pharisees. He called them hypocrites, blind guides, killers, fools, and summed them up in Matthew 23:33 as,

> *Ye serpents, ye generation of vipers, how can ye escape the damnation of hell?* (Matthew 23:33).

Would you argue with Him and say, "I just don't like the way you said that, Lord." I think not!

Finally, I believe the question which *should* be asked is, "How could I <u>not</u> write this book?"

Dr. Max D. Younce

Chapter One

Martin Luther's "Ten" Commandments

Luther did not believe all of God's Ten Commandments, as recorded in Exodus 20:2-17 and Deuteronomy 5:6-21. Both Exodus and Deuteronomy list the Ten in the same order. Luther did not believe the Second Commandment, so he omitted it in his Large and *Small Catechism.* Therefore, to show *ten* commandments in his Catechisms after eliminating the Second, he then takes the Tenth Commandment and divides it in two, showing it as number Nine and number Ten. Wherever the Ten Commandments are on public display in our country, they are always in the same order, and the same ones as given in the Word of God. In order to prepare you for this deceit, Martin Luther states on Page 44 of *The Small Catechism* the following:

> **NOTE: "The Lord gave the Ten Commandments, but He did not say which is the First, the Second, the Third, etc. Not all churches use the same order in numbering the Commandments."**

This statement is to cover Luther's deceit, should you notice in his Catechism that the Second Commandment of the Bible is ***omitted*** by Luther. He then takes the Third Commandment and lists it as the Second Commandment. Very sneaky actions for a man who claimed to believe God's Word!

Now, let's go to Exodus 20:1-3 and notice in Verse 3 which commandment God gives first. *"And God spake all these words, saying, I am the LORD thy God, which have brought thee out of the land of Egypt, out of the house of bondage."* (Exodus 20:1,2). In Verse 3, he gives the First Commandment. *"Thou shalt have no other gods before me."*

In refutation of Luther's statement on Page 44 of his *Small Catechism*, why would God have to say this is the First Commandment when it is the First Commandment God gave. In order to hide from you the fact he did not believe the Second Commandment, Luther further states that, "Not all churches use the same order in numbering the Commandments."

Of course, Luther fails to name any specific church or churches that change the order of the Ten Commandments. You are just supposed to believe Luther *because Luther said it*, with no documentation. Why would any Bible-believing church change the order of the commandments, from the order in which God gave them? Maybe God should have consulted with Luther to see if He was doing it right. All of this is Luther's smoke-screen to cover up your perception of his unbelief in God's Second Commandment, which he omitted in his Catechisms.

Let's look again at Luther's statement on Page 44 of his *Small Catechism* where he states that "God did not say which is the First, the Second, the Third Commandment and etc." Yet, Luther on Page 5 (*Small Catechism*) lists the First Commandment as the First Commandment that God gave.

"Thou shalt have no other gods before me." (Exodus 20:3). Knowing this, the next commandment in Verses 4-6 would be the Second Commandment. Then follows the Third Commandment in Verse 7 which states: *"Thou shalt not take the name of the LORD thy God in vain.* (Exodus 20:7.)*"*

- ***Luther's First Lie.***

Notice, on Page 5 of *The Small Catechism*, he takes the Third Commandment and tells you it is the Second Commandment. This is Luther's first lie in the deception of getting you to believe him instead of believing God's Word concerning the Ten Commandments.

- ***The Second Lie.***

In Exodus 20:5, God said the Fourth Commandment is, *"Remember the Sabbath day and keep it holy."* Luther says this is the Third Commandment. (*Small Catechism*, Page 5).

- ***The Third Lie.***

In Exodus 20:12, God said the Fifth Commandment is *"honour thy father and thy mother."* Luther says this is the Fourth Commandment. (*Small Catechism*, Page 6).

- ***The Fourth Lie.***

In Exodus 20:13, God said the Sixth Commandment is, *"Thou shalt not kill."* Luther says this is the Fifth Commandment. (*Small Catechism*, Page 6).

- ***The Fifth Lie.***

In Exodus 20:14, God said the Seventh Commandment is, *"Thou shalt not commit adultery."* Luther said this is the Sixth Commandment. (*Small Catechism*, Page 6).

- ***The Sixth Lie.***

In Exodus 20:15, God said the Eighth Commandment is, *"Thou shalt not steal."* Luther said, "This is the Seventh Commandment." (*Small Catechism*, Page 6).

- ***The Seventh Lie.***

In Exodus 20:16, God said the Ninth Commandment is *"Thou shalt not bear false witness against they neighbor."* Luther said, this is the Eighth Commandment (*Small Catechism*, Page 7).

- ***The Eighth Lie.***

In Exodus 20:17, God said the Tenth Commandment is, *"Thou shalt not covet thy neighbor's wife, nor his man servant, nor his maidservant, nor his ox, nor his ass, nor any thing that is thy neighbor's."* Luther divides this verse and says this is Commandments Number Nine and Ten. (*Small Catechism*, Page 7).

The Second Commandment, which Luther omitted, and did not believe, is found in Exodus 20:4-6.

> *"Thou shalt not make unto thee any graven image, or any likeness of anything that is in heaven above, or that is in the earth beneath, or that is in the water under the earth:* (V.4).
>
> *Thou shalt not bow down thyself to them, nor serve them: for I the LORD thy God am a jealous God, visiting the iniquity of the fathers upon the children unto the third and fourth generation of them that hate me;* (V.5).
>
> *And showing mercy unto thousands of them that love me, and keep my commandments."*(V.6).

Luther believed and followed the Roman Catholic organization in bowing to images made of Mary and various other "saints." This is why Luther did not believe the Second Commandment and excluded it from his Catechism. You talk about hypocrites and deceitful men concerning the Bible, Martin Luther is the *Master of Deceit!*

Now let us examine what Luther says on Page 8 of his *Small Catechism*.

> **"What does God say of <u>ALL</u> these commandments?**

By making the statement "all these commandments," you are being led to believe that the Ten Commandments in Luther's Small Catechism, Pgs. 5-7, are the same as given by God in Exodus 20. If Luther had been an honest man, he would have come out in a straightforward manner in his Catechism and told his followers, "I do not believe in God's Second Commandment; therefore, I have excluded it from *my* Ten Commandments." At least we could respect him for being honest with himself and his followers.

Luther continues on Page 8, Paragraph 2, of *The Small Catechism*, to warn his followers that,

> **"God threatens to punish all that transgress these commandments."**

In this statement by Luther, he condemns himself! He is the one who disbelieves the Second Commandment and excludes it from his Catechism.

This man has little respect for the *intelligence* of his followers as will be seen by his next step of deception. If you have a *Small Catechism*, I hope you will turn to Page 8, Paragraph 1, and notice what Luther quotes from the Bible, which is the Second Commandment as found in Exodus 20:4-6. *Remember*, this is the Commandment he excluded and did not believe. The following is the Second Commandment in its entirety from the Bible. What is **underlined** is what Luther only quoted in his Catechism. What is **not underlined** is what he did not believe.

> *"Thou shalt not make unto thee any graven image, or any likeness of any thing that is in heaven above, or that is in the earth beneath, or that is in the water under the earth:"* (Exodus 20:4).

> *"Thou shalt not bow down thyself to them, nor serve them: for I the LORD thy God am a jealous God,*

visiting the iniquity of the fathers upon the children unto the third and fourth generation of them that hate me; (Exodus 20:5). *And showing mercy unto thousands of them that love me, and keep my commandments."* (Exodus 20:6).

Luther does not believe all of Verse 4 in Exodus, Chapter 20, and believes only part of Verse 5, as he omitted 47 words from the Second Commandment. In other words, Luther says he believes God's judgment will be upon those who do not believe in the Second Commandment, which includes himself. Notice Verse 5, how that Luther does not believe the first half of the verse; but, says he believes the latter part, which he quotes on Page 8. (*Small Catechism*).

James 1:8 describes Luther precisely, *"A double-minded man is unstable in all his ways."* The Word of God in Proverbs 30:5 tells us that, *"Every word of God is pure..."* Luther, by excluding the Second Commandment, does not believe these words. Luther only picks and chooses which parts of the Bible he wants to believe to endorse his philosophy.

I have talked to many, many Lutherans and I have yet to find one who is aware of Luther's disbelief and exclusion of the Second Commandment from his Catechism. Sad to say, they don't even care. Luther has been dead for about 460 years, and his false teachings are as much alive today as they were when he was living. This is only one of the many false teachings and deceptions of Luther. We will continue to explore them one by one.

One must remember that in 1508 Luther was appointed to a university in Wittenberg, Germany, as a public teacher of Philosophy. Notice Colossians 2:8,

> *"Beware lest any man spoil you through philosophy and vain deceit, after the tradition of men, after the rudiments of the world, and not after Christ."*

Yes, Luther is unquestionably the *"Master of Deceit."* Notice on Page 41, Paragraph 11 (*Small Catechism*) Luther's words. "***Every*** word of the Bible is God's word, and therefore the Bible is without error." Luther lied in this statement in deleting the Second Commandment from his Catechism, which contains 91 words. Judge for yourself. Does Luther love God and believe that every word of the Bible is God's Word, or is he a liar and a false teacher?

Before I conclude this chapter, I would like it known that I am trusting Jesus Christ as the One who was crucified, buried, and rose again, paying for my sins on the cross. Acts 4:12 states,

> *"Neither is there salvation in any other: for there is none other name under heaven given among men, whereby we must be saved."*

For this reason, I know I have everlasting life with the Lord in heaven as promised in John 3:36.

> *"He that believeth on the Son hath everlasting life: and he that believeth not the Son shall not see life; but the wrath of God abideth on him."*

Luther believes (*Large Catechism*, Page 85, Par. 41) that water baptism promises and brings:

1. **Victory over death and the devil**
2. **Forgiveness of sins**
3. **God's grace**
4. **The entire Christ**
5. **The Holy Spirit with His gifts**

We will cover this, and more, in our coming examination of Luther, the Master of Deceit." I feel, as Joshua did in Joshua 24:15, *"As for me and my house, we will serve the Lord."* Not Martin Luther.

Chapter Two

Infant Baptism

Four Lies Used By Martin Luther To Perpetrate His False Doctrine of Infant Baptism.

Due to the many questions concerning Luther's teaching that infants are to be baptized, as projected in his *Large* and *Small Catechisms*; his philosophy deserves an answer from the Word of God. These questions come from sincere people who, from a child, have been raised and indoctrinated in the Catechism of Luther's philosophy.

In witnessing to many Lutherans, I have found they will believe the Catechism over the Bible. It appears that any teaching which contradicts their Catechism is considered a cult religion. In Psalms 118:8, the middle verse of the Bible, is a warning to all humanity, *"It is better to trust in the LORD than to put confidence in man."* (This includes Martin Luther!).

Jeremiah 17:5 gives the same warning. *"Thus saith the LORD; Cursed be the man that trusteth in man, and maketh flesh his arm, and whose heart departeth from the LORD."*

May I point out that Luther had *many false beliefs*! He did not believe in the Rapture; nor the 70th Week of Daniel, known as the 7-Year Tribulation Period; nor the Restoration of the Nation of Israel; nor the 1,000 Year Kingdom Reign of Christ on the earth. He had a difficult time reconciling the Epistle of James with the Book of

Romans; therefore, calling the Book of James, "the epistle of straw" and etc.

In this chapter, the examination of Martin Luther's teachings will be confined specifically to that of Infant Baptism.

In the following I will present to the reader the verses of Scripture that Luther gives in his *Small Catechism* as his so-called proof that infants are to be baptized. If you want to know the truth, I would strongly suggest that you get your Bible out, along with *Luther's Small Catechism* and follow along in our information. If not, then I agree with God's Word in I Corinthians 14:38, *"If any man be ignorant, let him be ignorant."*

- ***Luther's First Lie of Deceit: Infants Should Be Baptized As They Are Part Of "All Nations."***

In *Luther's Small Catechism*, P. 173, #251, he states,

"How do you prove that infants, too, are to be baptized?"

Then he continues,

"Infants, too, are to be baptized—because they are included in the words "all nations."

Then he quotes Matthew 28:19 as proof.

"Go ye therefore and TEACH all nations, baptizing them in the name of the Father and of the Son and of the Holy Ghost."

Luther says that "all nations" is inclusive of infants. Notice that this verse says to TEACH all nations. How is a person going to teach an infant the Word of God, when they can't walk, talk, understand, or even say "Goo! Goo!"

Now let us get the Greek word for "infant." The Greek is "*BREPHOS*" and is translated "*infants*" in Luke 18:15; and also as "*babe*" in Luke 2:12,16. Will you please tell me how an INFANT can be taught, whose mind has not yet developed to the point of understanding any words?

Now we are going to examine the word "TEACH" and you will see for yourself how deceitful Luther really is. The Greek word for "TEACH" is the verb "*MATHETEUO*," and means, "*to make disciples.*" The Greek noun for "*disciple*" is "*MATHETES*" and means, "*a learner, to learn, indicating thought accompanied by endeavor.* (*Vine's Expository Dictionary of Greek New Testament Words*). This is *impossible* with an infant.

Luther knew that no infant could be taught to be a disciple, so he purposely chose to deceive you by not revealing that the Greek word "*MATHETEUO*" means "make disciples" and should have been translated thus. If you still have any doubt about Luther's deception; remember, he knew the Greek well as he translated it into the German Language Bible.

Go back with me now in his *Small Catechism* to P.171, #619, and notice he quotes the same verse, Matthew 28:19 and puts after the word "TEACH. **"[*make disciples of*]."**

If brought to justice, Luther would be charged with criminal deceit, found guilty by his own Catechism, and sentenced to bear the title publicly of "The Master of Deceit." Luther had previously been injected with the "serpent's venom" of Catholicism, concerning infant baptism. Luther refused the antidote, the Word of God, to free himself from this damnable doctrine of baptismal regeneration of infants. Luther should have acknowledged Psalm 118:8 and Jeremiah 17:5, and obeyed what God has said.

> *"It is better to trust in the LORD than to put confidence in man." (Psalms 118:8).*
>
> *"Thus saith the LORD; Cursed be the man that trusteth in man, and maketh flesh his arm, and whose heart departeth from the LORD."* (Jeremiah 17:5).

- ***Luther's Second Lie of Deceit: Infants Can Be Born Again.***

Go with me now to *Luther's Small Catechism*, P.173, under B. Here are Luther's words concerning Infant Baptism.

> **"Because <u>Holy</u> Baptism is the only means whereby infants, who, too, must be born**

> **again, can ordinarily be regenerated and brought to faith."**

After reading Luther's words, allow me to ask you a very simple question. Can you pick out the LIE Luther just put forth in this statement to deceive you? What about the words "***Holy*** Baptism"? Do you know that "Holy Baptism" is found nowhere in the Bible? God never had the Holy Spirit inspire any writer to record the words "Holy" Baptism."

Baptism is only a public testimony, outwardly showing that my faith is in the death and resurrection of Jesus Christ, who paid for my sins and assured me of everlasting life. (John 3:16, 36). The reason Luther added "Holy" to baptism was to deceive you into believing his philosophy, that baptism saves you. Here are Luther's words in his *Large Catechism*, P. 83, #24.

> **"To put it most simply, the power, effect, benefit, fruit, and purpose of Baptism IS TO SAVE."**

Now since Luther added the word "Holy" to baptism, let us see what God has to say about Luther.

> *"Add thou not unto his words, lest he reprove thee, and thou (Luther) be found a liar."* (Proverbs 30:6).

God says Luther is charged with deceit, lying, and adding his philosophy (i.e.,"Holy" baptism); thus, tampering with the Word of God. "Guilty" is God's verdict and

Luther is sentenced to carry his banner publicly, identifying him as the "Master of Deceit."

- ***Luther's Third Lie of Deceit: He Ignores the Greek Words for "Young Children" And "Infants."***

In Luther's support of his belief that infants are to be baptized to inherit eternal life, he quotes, Mark 10:13-15 (*Luther's Small Catechism*, P.173, #625).

> *"And they brought young children to him; that he should touch them: and his disciples rebuked those that brought them." (V.13).*
>
> *"But when Jesus saw it, he was much displeased, and said unto them. Suffer the little children to come unto me, and forbid them not: for of such is the kingdom of God. (V.14).*
>
> *"Verily I say unto you, whosoever shall not receive the kingdom of God as a little child, he shall not enter therein." (V.15).*

Let us analyze these verses and see if Luther's claim is valid, or if it is another attempt to deceive you.

First, I don't see anything in these verses that has to do with infants. The Greek word for "infants," also translated "babe" or "baby" is "*BREPHOS*." This Greek word appears nowhere in Mark 10:13-15.

Secondly, Where does it say anything about BAPTISM in these verses? Will you show me anywhere in

God's Word where Christ ever baptized anyone, let alone babies; or, where, in the Bible, do we ever find that a baby (infant) was ever baptized?

Notice in Verse 15, *"Whosoever shall not receive the kingdom of God as a little child, he shall not enter therein."* A little child is capable of believing; but, not an infant! I know many, many Christian parents whose children have trusted Christ as their Savior as young as four and five years of age. No infant is capable of understanding that Jesus died on the cross and was resurrected to pay for their sins. This is an abstract concept which the infantile mind cannot understand.

In Verse 15, the minds of these little children had not been corrupted with the philosophy of false teachers, such as the atheists, agnostics, evolutionists, and God-haters. Therefore, their minds are free from the pollution of the false teaching of Satan's ambassadors. Thus, when the truth of God's Word is presented and taught to them, that Jesus loves them and paid for their sins; they simply believe it and are saved. This is the foundation they will have for the rest of their life.

On the other hand, should a child grow up in a godless home, that influence may be adapted into their thinking and behavior. Of course, Satan will do all he can to insure that a person does not believe that Jesus Christ is their Savior. II Corinthians 4:3,4 bears this out.

> *"But if our gospel be hid, it is hid to them that are lost." (V. 3).*

> *"In whom the god of this world (Satan) hath blinded the minds of them which believe not, lest the light of the glorious gospel of Christ, who is the image of God, should shine unto them." (V.4)*

As one gets older, their mind is now infiltrated with all kinds of lies concerning the Bible, the Word of God. Then one is encountered by a Christian who witnesses to him how that God loves him, and Jesus Christ came to this earth, died on the cross, and was resurrected as payment for his sin. So the question, referring back to Verse 15 is, How does this man "*receive the kingdom of God* (i.e. everlasting life) *as a little child*"?

The answer is very simple. A child's mind is clean and free from anything that contradicts the Word of God. Therefore, the child simply believes that "*...God so loved the world, that he gave his only begotten Son* (Jesus Christ*), that whosoever believeth in him should not perish, but have everlasting life.*" (John 3:16). The child is saved.

How does the older man become as a little child to inherit the kingdom of God? He changes his mind and frees it by believing the Bible to be true (just as a small child); and by discarding the philosophies and ideologies of God-haters as nothing more than Satanic lies. He has now "flushed his mind clean" (as a little child) and simply believes that Jesus Christ died for him personally and rose again in payment for his sins. He is now saved as promised by John 5:24, the same as a young child.

> *"Verily, Verily, I say unto you, He that heareth my word, and believeth on him that sent me, hath*

everlasting life, and shall not come into condemnation; but is passed from death unto life."

It amazes me that Luther, the one who claims to take only Scripture as his authority, would believe and teach Infant Baptism, when it is found nowhere in the Bible. Then he uses Mark 10:13-15 as his endorsement to deceive his followers. These verses have no reference at all to infants; neither do these verses say anything about baptism.

Luther's philosophy of infant baptism disintegrates when compared to the Word of God; yet, Satan has protected and projected this damnable lie for over 460 years to our present time. Today we are saturated in certain areas with "Luther's puppets" behind the pulpit projecting Satan's lie of infant baptism.

Remember, all false teaching flows from the throne of Satan, who hates the Word of God. Luther is unquestionably "the Master of Deceit." Notice the Holy Spirit's warning in II Corinthians 11:14,15.

> *"And no marvel: for Satan himself is transformed into an angel of light. Therefore is it no great thing if his (Satan's) ministers also be transformed as the ministers of righteousness..."*

Luther was blinded to the very simple teaching of God's Word and the lessons which follow as recorded in Mark 10:13-15. Analyze for yourself the following:

- "*Young*" and "*little children*" **are not** "*infants;*" but children who are capable of understanding who Jesus is. (The Greek for "*infant*" is "*BREPHOS*," which does not appear anywhere in these verses.)

- ❖ The parents brought their young children to Christ so that he would "*touch*" them. Why would they do this? These parents were, no doubt, part of the people Christ had previously taught and who had also witnessed people being healed by Him later near the River Jordan. (Matthew 19:1,2 and Mark 10:1, same account). They believed Christ was the Messiah, the Son of God and was soon going to be crucified, resurrected, and ascend back to Heaven. What a thrill for these children to be able to tell their children that Jesus, the Savior, had actually laid His hands on them as a gesture of His love for them. (Matthew 19:15).

- ❖ In Verse 14, Jesus said concerning the children, *"for **of such** is the kingdom of God."* In other words, these children were saved and already a part of the Kingdom of God. Our Lord Jesus Christ just said so! They believed that Jesus was their Savior, because their PARENTS, who were believers, had taught them. That is why they brought their children to see Christ. Take notice that there is no record anywhere in the Word of God that these children had been baptized, yet they possessed eternal life in the Kingdom of God.

God's instructions all through the Old and New Testaments are directed to the parents to ***teach*** their children (not infants) the Word of God. Note: You will find nowhere in the Bible where God ever instructs parents to teach their infants. Notice the following, for example:

- Ephesians 6:4 – Training "*children,*" not infants.
- Colossians 3:21 – "*Children,*" not infants.
- Deuteronomy 6:6,7 – Teach "*children,*" not infants.
- Deuteronomy 11:18,19 – Teach "*children,*" not infants.
- Deuteronomy 31:12, 13 – "*Children*" twice, not infants.
- Psalm 78:5 – "*Children*", not infants.
- Proverbs 22:6 – "*Train up a child*" not infants.
- Proverbs 29:15 – "*Child,*" not infants.

None of the above references are to "teach" or "train" infants. The Greek word for "*infants*" is not used in Ephesians 6:4 or Colossians 3:21. The Hebrew for "infant" is "*OWLEL*" and is absent in the above Old Testament references to teaching children, not infants. Infants are incapable of understanding or reasoning.

You have a choice. Are you going to believe the lies and deceit of Luther who has been dead for over 460 years, or the Lord Jesus Christ? Christ said, *"I am the way, the truth, and the life and no man cometh unto the Father but by me."* (John 14:6).

> *"These things have I written unto you that believe on the name of the Son of God; that ye may know that ye have eternal life, and that ye may believe on the name of the Son of God."* (I John 5:13).

- ***Luther's Fourth Lie of Deceit: Infants, Too, Can Believe.***

On P.174 C. in *Luther's Small Catechism*, he states, "**Because infants, too, can believe**." Then he quotes as his support Matthew 18;6, which states:

> *"But whoso shall offend one of these little ones which believe in me, it were better for him that a millstone were hanged about his neck and that he were drowned in the depth of the sea."*

Notice the words *"these little ones which believe."* The Greek word for "little" here is "*MIKROS*," an adjective meaning "*little or small,*" NOT an infant. Furthermore, nowhere in this verse do we find anything about baptism; yet, Luther wants you to believe his philosophy about infant baptism, which is absolutely contradictory to this verse. This was not an oversight by Luther; but, *purposely* done to deceive his followers. One must remember that Luther knew the Greek language well in order to translate the Bible into the German language. Therefore, he knew the word *"MIKROS"* means "little or small," and is never translated "infants" in the Bible.

If I could talk with Martin Luther today, I would ask him these questions. "Why, Mr. Luther, were you not honest in telling your followers about the meaning of the word "*mikros*" in your Catechism? You purposely lied to all who follow *your* teaching instead of the Word of God. You were indoctrinated by the Roman Catholic organization and carried this lie of infant baptismal regeneration with you to your death in 1546!

You have led people by the thousands to believe that their infant child is now going to heaven because your preachers have sprinkled a few drops of water on their head. What an insult to God! In other words, if a baby (infant) isn't baptized, then it will go to Hell!"

In talking to hundreds of Catholics and Lutherans, it is unthinkable that they actually believe that God would send an infant to Hell! Let me give you just one example out of thousands.

A man and his wife came to our church on several occasions. We were invited to their home to visit. This was a nice young couple who were expecting their first child shortly, and her parents were Lutherans. The subject of the baptism of babies came up in the conversation and I related to her that nowhere does the Bible say that babies are ever to be baptized. I will never forget her statement, "Oh, my mother will throw a fit!" Here, a Grandmother wanted to make sure the baby would go to Heaven by being baptized.

Where did this false teaching originate? From a dead man's writings, by the name of Luther, some 460 years ago in his Catechisms. The end of the story is this. They never came back to church again. Why? All because of the heresy of Luther's damnable doctrine of infant baptism, passed on down from one generation to another.

Nowhere in the Bible do you ever find that God puts infants in Hell if they are not baptized. Don't you think that if God sent infants to Hell, He would at least put *ONE* verse in the entire Bible stating, "Be sure and have your infants baptized or I will send them to Hell!" How absurd!

Remember, Luther knew the Hebrew and Greek languages well, in order to translate the Bible into the German language. Therefore, when he used Matthew 18:6, he knew *"BREPHOS,"* the Greek word for "infant" was not in this verse. This was a premeditated deceit done by Luther in an attempt to align your thinking with his philosophy. I might say, he has been very successful over the last 460 years.

God describes how Luther and *every* false teacher accomplishes their goals in Romans 16:18, *"For they that are such serve not our Lord Jesus Christ,* (although they pretend to) *but their own belly* (i.e., their own inward thoughts and desires)*; and by GOOD WORDS and FAIR SPEECHES* ***deceive*** *the hearts of the simple."*

Luther's use of Matthew 18:6 to support his philosophy of infant baptism would constitute his Fourth Lie of Deception. In a criminal court of law, the guilty party, Martin Luther, would be considered a repeat offender, or as an habitual law breaker. In Ephesians 4:25 God sets forth His law about lying, *"Wherefore putting away lying, speak every man truth with his neighbor..."* Therefore, Luther will have to be indicted and face charges of breaking God's law against lying; perverting God's word by deception, and being a habitual offender along with premeditation. The verdict is "Guilty!"

The sentencing is as follows. The public should be notified of the charges against him as a result of his attempt to deceive the <u>simple</u> (i.e., those that are innocent and unsuspecting of Luther's devices). He will bear publicly the title he deserves, the "Master of Deceit!"

The decision a person is faced with is, "Will I believe the philosophy and words of Luther, a man who has been dead for 460 years; or, the words of God who is alive and well today?" The One who is your Creator, and the One who loves you and gave His only begotten Son to pay for your sins and mine on the cross, states in Proverbs 30:5, *"Every word of God is pure: he is a shield unto them that put their TRUST in him."* Not, Martin Luther!.

One must remember that Luther did nothing more than follow the tradition of the Roman Catholic organization. In the Catechism of the Roman Catholic Church, P. 319, Par.1252, they state, "The practice of Infant Baptism is an *immemorial* TRADITION of the Church."

The definition of "immemorial" is, "extending back beyond memory, record, or knowledge." (Webster's Encyclopedic Unabridged Dictionary of the English Language.) This simply means that the Catholic organization has no memory of *when* this started. They have no record of *who* made this up, they have no knowledge of *where* it came from. They just decided to baptize babies and, then, labeled it as a *"tradition."* This is proof they do not believe God's Word in Proverbs 30:6 which states,

> *"Add thou not unto his words, lest he reprove thee, and thou be found a liar."* (Proverbs 30:6).

Luther has followed a tradition of the Roman Catholic organization and now his "puppet" preachers have perpetrated this same traditional lie for some 460 years upon the innocent and unsuspecting.

- ***Does God Ever Send Infants To Hell?***

We have no record in God's word that infants ever are sent to Hell because they are not baptized. In talking to many Lutherans, over the years, I have asked them, "*Why* did you have your baby baptized?" Most usually, I received one or more of the following answers:

- ❖ "I don't want my baby going to Hell."
- ❖ "I want to make sure my baby is going to Heaven."
- ❖ "I am not taking any chances.
- ❖ "It is better to do it, than not to do it."
- ❖ "This is what our church believes."
- ❖ "Our pastor wouldn't tell us to do it, if it wasn't in the Bible."

And on, and on it goes.

The root of this heresy comes from *their* "god," the founder of their sect, Martin Luther. By the way, "heresy" in the Bible comes from the Greek word, "hairesis," and means "*an opinion, especially a self-willed opinion, which is substituted for submission to the power of truth, and leads to division and the formation of sects.*" *Vines Expository Dictionary of Greek New Testament Words.*

- ***Luther Believes Unbaptized Infants Cannot "Enter...The Kingdom of God."***

Here are Luther's own words in his Catechism,

> **"Because Holy Baptism is the only means whereby infants, who, too, must be born again..."** (*Small Catechism*, P.173 B).

In support of this on Page 174, Paragraph 626, he quotes John 3:5,6.

> *"...Except a man be born of water and of the Spirit, he cannot enter into the kingdom of God; that which is born of the flesh is flesh..."*

Very simply put, Luther believes that infants *must be baptized*; or they *cannot* enter the kingdom of God. If an infant is not baptized and it cannot enter the kingdom of God, according to Luther; then, Hell is the only *other* destination. When people follow Luther, is it any wonder that I received the answers I did as to why people wanted to have their babies baptized?

Did you ever wonder why Luther did not come right out, in a straightforward manner, and plainly say, "Unbaptized babies will go to Hell?" The reason is, he knew it was not true as there is no Scripture to support such an accusation against God. Only by inference could Luther inject this into the minds of his followers. Therefore, if only baptized infants go to Heaven; then, it is inferred by deductive reasoning that unbaptized babies go to Hell, and Luther did not have to come out and say so directly. Pretty slick!

Before I continue, I want to bring out a few things concerning this false teaching to stimulate your thinking:

- Read all of John, Chapter 3, and you will find there is nothing mentioned about water baptism whatsoever!

- The "*kingdom of God*" and "*everlasting life*" are synonymous words. Both are conditioned upon believing, not being baptized!

  "Thy kingdom is an everlasting kingdom." (Psalm 145:13).

- Almost every time Luther sees the word "water," his brain "computes" it into baptism; thus, disregarding the context.

- The word "*water*" in John 3:5,6 has reference to the Word of God, not baptism. (Ephesians 5:26; John 17:3).

  "Being born again, not of corruptible seed (i.e., any work of the flesh)*, but of incorruptible, by the word of God, which liveth and abideth forever."*(I Peter 1:23).

- Luther says that infants receive the Holy Spirit at baptism. Here are Luther's words:

  "Now, if God did not accept the Baptism of infants, he would not have given any of them the Holy Spirit, nor any part of him." (Large Catechism, P. 86, 87, Par. 49,50**).**

This is an outright lie, *meant* to deceive! According to the Bible, only those capable of believing are given the Holy Spirit. Infants are incapable of this.

Let us go to the Bible and see God's refutation of Luther's lie. In Ephesians 1:13b we are told that *"...the gospel of your salvation: in whom* ***also after that ye believed,*** *ye were sealed with that Holy Spirit of promise."* So, I ask, how can an infant receive the Holy Spirit when they are incapable of believing?

- ❖ Nowhere are infants included in John 3:5,6. Christ is talking with an adult man, the Pharisee, Nicodemus. Infants are not mentioned.

- ❖ In Luther's *Large* and *Small Catechisms*, within the "Baptism" sections, notice how many times Luther uses the words "Holy Baptism" to deceive you. This is found NOWHERE in the Bible. Luther has gone to great lengths to deceive his followers concerning infant baptism. He should be "recognized" for his achievements by the title he deserves, the "Master of Deceit."

We will expound on John 3:1-8 later on in examining Luther's lies concerning baptismal regeneration for adults.

- ***Babies (Infants) That Die, Immediately Enter The Kingdom of God, Entering Into The Presence of Jesus Christ In Heaven.***

When a child is born, it is born with a sinful nature. (Romans 3:23). As the body, soul, and spirit of that infant grow together, the child will reach the time when it can reason, understand, think for itself, and make decisions concerning what is right and what is wrong. At that time, the child will be responsible for those decisions. The development of this mental awareness can vary a great deal from child to child. When that child becomes accountable to the Lord is determined by God, Himself, who is omniscient, or all-knowing. God is the only One who can look into the mind of every person in His creation and determine when that person is of age, mentally, to give an account of themselves.

Notice in I Samuel 16:7b, ***"For the LORD seeth not as man seeth; for man looketh on the outward appearance, but the LORD looketh on the HEART."*** The word of God in Hebrews 4:13b states that the Lord "***is a discerner of the thoughts and intents of the heart.***" This is God's judgment and we can rest assured, it is without error!

- ***How We Know Unbaptized Babies Go To Heaven.***

  - ***The Death of An Infant.***

Now let us go back and center our thoughts on an infant who has died. A very sad thing to consider, I assure you; but, since that infant is incapable of knowing anything, let alone committing a sin; therefore, we can conclude that the infant is innocent and free from committing any sin at all. Christ, Himself, makes it perfectly clear that this infant will be carried by the angels into the presence of the Lord, in the Kingdom of God.

You will recall, in Luke 16:22, we have recorded the death of Lazarus, the beggar. *"And it came to pass, that the beggar died (Lazarus), and was* ***carried by the angels*** *into Abraham's bosom...*(i.e. another term for 'Paradise')." When one considers the thousands of deaths that occur all over the world in just one day, it gives an idea of how busy some of God's angels are. However, we can rest assured they are equal to the job, as God's Word says they are "innumerable." (Hebrews 12:22).

❖ *Infants Are Part of the Kingdom of God.*

Christ lets us know that *all infants*, because they have never sinned, and are incapable of knowing anything, are part of the Kingdom of God. Christ, Himself, gives us the absolute assurance of this in Luke 18:15,16,

> *"And they brought unto him* (Christ) *also INFANTS* (Greek "brephos"), *that he would touch them: but when his disciples saw it, they rebuked them. But Jesus called them unto him, and said, Suffer* (i.e. allow) *little children to come unto me, and forbid them not: for of such is the kingdom of God."*

This assurance is from the lips of our Wonderful Savior, the Lord Jesus Christ, Himself!

Should a baby die due to some disease; or maybe crib death; or as the result of an unfortunate accident of some sort; that would be heartbreaking to the parents and almost unbearable. Christ's assurance to the parents and loved ones is that their baby, upon death of the body, is itself carried by God's angels into the very presence of Christ, Himself, in the Kingdom of God.

Yes, there *is* great sorrow; but, having the peace of knowing their child is in Heaven with the Lord is a great consolation and comfort. As Christian parents, they know they will see and be with their child again. It is not "Good Bye," BUT, only, "So long for a while."

❖ ***From The Example of David's Son.***

In II Samuel, Chapters 11 and 12, God records the tragedy of King David having Uriah, the husband of Bath-sheba, killed. David did this to conceal the fact that he had committed adultery with Bathsheba and she was now *"with child."* God's judgment is recorded in II Samuel 12:14,

> *"Howbeit, because by this deed thou* (David) *hast given great occasion to the enemies of the LORD to blaspheme, the child also that is born unto thee shall surely die."*

II Samuel 12:18 tells us that the child was only seven days old when it died. *"And it came to pass on the seventh day, that the child died."* This baby had not been baptized; yet, it went to Paradise, which was within the Kingdom of God. Notice David's steadfast assurance that he would see his son again, as stated in II Samuel 12:23,

> *"But now he is dead, wherefore should I fast? Can I bring him back again? I shall go to him, but he shall not return to me."*

Most all Christians are well familiar with the Twenty-Third Psalm, written by King David. Notice care-fully Verse 6, which is the last verse.

> *"Surely goodness and mercy shall follow me all the days of my life: and I will dwell in the house of the LORD for ever."* (Psalms 23:6).

David knew that, when he died, he would dwell in the *"house of the Lord"* forever. The only way David could make this statement in full assurance, that "*I shall go to him*" in II Samuel 12:23 is, he *knew* his son would be in the *"house of the Lord,"* i.e., the same place David would go upon his death. Therefore, the only way he could go to be with his son is, if they were both in the ***same*** place!

May I draw your attention back to Luke 18:15,16, where INFANTS were brought to Christ and He assured the parents, and all present, *"for* ***of such*** *is the kingdom of God."* David's son of seven days old, died; but, went to dwell in the *"house of the Lord,"* this being synonymous with *"the kingdom of God."*

David's infant of 7 days old was never baptized. Neither were the infants in Luke 18. Nowhere in the whole Bible can you find one case where an infant was ever baptized. How seductive the power of Satan is seen in the Catholic organization, and in the teachings of Martin Luther and his "puppet" preachers in setting up a false "savior" of baptismal waters; instead, of the blood sacrifice of Christ, *"who liveth and abideth forever."*

Remember, the difference between believing Martin Luther or Jesus Christ is Heaven, or Hell!

> *"It is better to trust in the Lord than to put confidence in man." (Psalm 118:8)*

Chapter Three

"THE TRAP DOOR TO HELL."
The Long Range Effect of Infant Baptism

The long range effect of infant baptism is nothing more than "The Trap Door to Hell." Allow me to qualify the preceding statement. In over 35 years in the ministry, I have witnessed to many, many Catholics and Lutherans. I am glad to say that I have led some of both to trust Christ, and Him alone, for their salvation. The sad part is that the majority, by far, reject Christ in lieu of dependence on their baptism and good works.

The baptism I am referring to is when their parents had them baptized as a baby. The good works are required as they grow up, showing that they are living out their baptism, **"which works forgiveness of sins, delivers from death and the Devil, and gives eternal salvation to all who believe this."** states Martin Luther.

Should one question the truth of the above, may I suggest that you open *Luther's Small Catechism*, P.174 under II entitled, **"The Blessings of Baptism,"** and read it for yourself. The sadness of this is, that the grown person has been taught since a child that, since they were baptized as a baby, they have eternal salvation. The church gives the parents a baptismal certificate, which is most often framed and cherished as a "Holy Writ." Later on, it is passed on to their children who reverence it as their "ticket" to Heaven!

The Heresies of Luther's Catechisms Live On

- ***Experiencing The Trap Door.***

I was out going door-to-door and came up to a man working in his yard. I introduced myself. As he was very friendly, I asked him a hypothetical question. "If you were to die tonight, do you know absolutely, positively, for sure you would go to Heaven?" His answer was, "I know I am going to Heaven and I have proof of it." I said, "That's great! What is your proof?"

I thought he would give me a verse of Scripture substantiating that his faith was in Jesus Christ as his Savior. To my disappointment, his proof was the following. "My parents had me baptized when I was three weeks old and that placed me into the family of God for my eternal life. I now have my baptismal certificate that was given to Mom and Dad when they had me baptized." He went on to say, "It is my most cherished possession." He said he had been raised Lutheran; but, I don't recall what sect it was.

This is an example of one of the results of Satan's workings through Luther in propagating the damnable doctrine of baptismal regeneration. II Corinthians 4:4 describes this man as one of Satan's victims.

> *"In whom the God of this world hath blinded the minds of them which believe not, lest the light of the glorious gospel of Christ, who is the image of God, should shine unto them."*

I tried to show this man in my Bible that Christ was the only way to Heaven (John 3:16,36 and John 14:6). He wanted nothing to do with the Bible and immediately became angry. His last response was, "Are you calling my Mom and Dad liars?" Are you saying my preacher is a liar and my church is no good?" At that point I was asked to leave and told not to come back. Not all my experiences in witnessing to this denomination have been this extreme; but, most will reject the blood of Christ shed upon Calvary in exchange for the waters of baptismal regeneration offered by Satan and his ministers.

The parents and this son were raised on the words of Luther's Catechism, instead of the living Word of God. Satan is very proud of Luther for the fine work he is doing through his Catechisms, which are still alive and active after 460 years. Through them, Satan is actively working to deceive as many people into Hell as he possibly can, and doing a very good job! What Satan offers through baptism is nothing more than a "Trap Door to Hell!" God describes Satan's ministers in II Corinthians 11:13-15:

> *"For such are false apostles, deceitful workers, transforming themselves into the apostles of Christ."*(V.13).
>
> *"And no marvel; for Satan himself is transformed into an angel of light."*(V.14).
>
> *"Therefore, it is no great thing if his ministers also be transformed as the ministers of righteousness; whose end shall be according to their works."*(V.15).

- ***The Trap Door Opens Again.***

Not long ago, I stopped at a certain residence to see if their children would like to go to camp with us. This is a yearly event in which we take kids to a Christian camp.

During our conversation the subject was brought up about babies being baptized, which the Mother endorsed. I related to her that nowhere in the Bible did God ever instruct parents to baptize babies and/or infants. She immediately stated that infants are included in Matthew 28:19 where the Bible says, *"Go ye therefore and teach all nations, baptizing them..."* I said to her, "Your pastor told you this, didn't he?" She hesitated briefly, then admitted that is where she got it.

I happened to have my brief case in my car with *Luther's Small Catechism* inside. I brought it out, and said to her, "I want to show you something and turned to Page 173 in the Small Catechism and read to her Luther's words concerning infants being baptized. His Scripture reference was Matthew 28:19 and his comments were stating that infants are included in "*all nations.*"

I told her this is where her pastor inherited this false teaching from Luther, who had been dead for some 460 years. "Now he has passed it on to you, and you are now passing it on to your children, who will probably pass it on to their children."

In reality, Luther is her god as she chooses to believe her pastor, who is a puppeteer pulling the strings of the congregation; therefore making *them* little puppets of

Luther. Luther is nothing more than an ambassador of Satan with his damnable philosophy of baptismal regeneration.

I also showed her that Luther knew that the word "*teach*" in this passage concerning "all nations," was the Greek word meaning "*make disciples of.*" Therefore, infants could not be included in "*all nations*" as you cannot make a disciple out of an infant who is not capable of conscious reasoning about anything. An infant recognizes blurry images of his mother and father, and responds to their loving touch; but, the infant cannot make decisions relating to the eternal destination of his or her soul.

The mother questioned this; but, in the *Small Catechism*, P.171, Par. 619, she could read where Luther placed in brackets after "*teach,*" the words [make disciples of]. All one has to do is read it for themselves!

Having no other argument to offer, her last response was that I was too blunt and was not a loving person. I asked her if she would promise me to read Matthew, Chapter 23. Then, I asked her if she was willing to tell Jesus that He is not a loving person when He told these religious leaders in Verse 33, "*Ye serpents, ye generation of vipers, how can ye escape the damnation of Hell?*"

The source of her religion can be traced back 460 years ago to a dead man by the name of Martin Luther. Millions and millions of people have been promised that baptism opened the doors to Heaven, only to find at the end of their life, it was the trap door to eternal Hell! Luther truly has earned the title of, "The Master of Deceit."

Chapter Four

Summary Of Luther's Philosophy of Infant Baptism.

- ***Infant Baptism Is Not Found In God's Word.***

You can search the Bible through, from Genesis to Revelation, and you will not find one case where an infant was ever baptized. Why didn't God instruct Adam and Eve to baptize their first two children, Cain and Abel? Why didn't God baptize Adam and Eve? After all, He created them, so it would not have been a problem to baptize them!

If, according to Luther, baptism gives eternal salvation, then God could have instructed Adam to baptize Eve; and, then Eve could have baptized Adam! But such was not the case. In Hebrews 9:22 we are told,

> *"And almost all things are by the law purged with blood; and without shedding of blood is no remission."*

❖ ***The First Mention Principle And The Sin of Adam and Eve.***

In Genesis 3:21, we find because of Adam and Eve's sin, innocent blood had to be shed.

> *"Unto Adam also and to his wife did the LORD God make coats of skins, and clothed them." (Genesis 3:21).*

Adam and Eve accepted the blood sacrifice that God had prepared and God then clothed them with the skins of innocent animals. This was only a "temporary fix," a covering only for the sin of Adam and Eve. This did not take away their sin, only covered it.

This is the first mention of "The Blood" in the Bible. It is known in Theology as the "First Mention Principle," in which God carries the same wave of truth throughout the rest of the Bible. *This* wave of truth culminated in the Lord Jesus Christ shedding His perfect, sinless blood on the cross of Calvary for the remission of all sins, for all humanity.

> *"The next day John seeth Jesus coming unto him, and saith, Behold the Lamb of God, which taketh away the sin of the world." (John 1:29).*

- ***Luther Has A Different Opinion! He Believes Water Baptism Can Take Away Sin, Or "The Way of Cain."***

In his *Small Catechism*, Page 174, #626 C., he states, ***"Because infants, too, can believe."*** Notice, at the bottom of the same page, Luther makes it perfectly clear what he is trusting for his salvation, and that is WATER BAPTISM! This includes infants also as he states, "Infants, too, can believe." How ridiculous and Satanic!

> **"II. The Blessings of Baptism. What does Baptism give or profit? It works forgiveness of sins, delivers from death and the devil, and gives eternal salvation to all who believe this, as the words and promises of God declare."**

Adam and Eve did not believe what Luther believes, as they taught Cain and Abel that God would only accept the blood sacrifice for the remission of their sins. Abel believed his parents, while Cain did not. In Genesis 4:4, Abel killed the lamb and offered the blood sacrifice which God accepted.

Cain, on the other hand, refused his parent's instructions and offered his own good works, pictured in the fruit of the ground. This was the seed he had sown, tended to, and harvested with his own hands. Can't you just see Cain as he artfully arranges his offering of fruits, vegetables, and grains, thinking to himself, "My offering is so much more beautiful than that bloody sacrifice of Abel's. Wait until God sees this!"

God rejected Cain's offering (Genesis 4:5-8), telling him it was a sinful offering. Cain was thinking that God would accept his good works as being sufficient, instead of the blood sacrifice being sufficient. God's words in Genesis 4:7 that "*sin lieth at the door*" infuriated Cain to the point of killing his brother, Abel. Cain was religious, or he wouldn't have brought *any* offering; but, it was a bloodless offering, centered only in his good works and self righteousness. In I John 3:12 we are told concerning Cain:

> *"Not as Cain, who was of that wicked one (Satan), and slew his brother (Abel). And wherefore slew he him? Because his own works were evil, and his brother's righteous."*

Is Martin Luther Any Different Than Cain? He, offers the work of baptism as the means of Salvation, therefore denying the FINISHED work of Christ on the cross. Christ last words on the cross are recorded in John 19:30,

> *"When Jesus therefore had received the vinegar, he said, It is finished: and he bowed his head and gave up the ghost."*

Luther never got his doctrine of infant baptism from the Bible; but, inherited this Satanic doctrine from the Roman Catholic organization.

- ***Four Examples To Provoke Your Thinking To Belief In God's Word.***

  - ***Abel*** was never baptized as an infant or as an adult. In Matthew 23:35, God said that Abel was a righteous man.

  - ***Noah*** was a preacher of righteousness (II Peter 2:5); but, was never baptized.

  - ***Enoch*** "who walked with God" and pleased God; but, was never baptized. (Hebrews 11:5; Genesis 5:24).

  - ***Abraham*** *"**believed** God and it was counted unto him for righteousness."* (Romans 4:3). Abraham was never baptized. These four examples are used only to direct your thinking to the Word of God, where no infant is ever recorded as being baptized; nor any parent ever instructed to baptize their infants.

- ***Would The Lord Condemn Little Infants To The Lake of Fire?***

Would one dare to think that the Lord, Who ***loves*** babies and little children, would actually place an infant in the Lake of Fire (Hell); because the parents did not have their baby baptized? May I draw your attention to Matthew 18:6, in which Christ ***expresses*** His love for little children.

> *"But whoso shall offend one of these little ones which BELIEVE IN ME, it were better for him that a millstone were hanged about his neck, and that he were drowned in the depth of the sea."*

Here, these little children were old enough to believe in Christ. They believed He was the Son of God, the Messiah who was going to the cross to pay for their sins and would be raised three days later, just as He had claimed. Should a skeptic or unbeliever mock or make fun of these little children who believed in Christ, He stated very clearly that it would be better for them to die physically once, than to die the second death and spend eternity in the Lake of Fire. With these words in mind from Christ, Himself, I ask you this question. "How could a person even entertain such a thought that Jesus would send an infant to eternal Hell, just because that infant didn't have a few drops of water sprinkled on his head by one of Luther's puppet preachers?"

Remember, an infant has not the mental faculties developed to even know what is right or wrong, or what the word "sin" means. An infant has not knowingly committed any sin. This infant can't even say, "Goo! Goo!" let alone know its parent's name. James 4:17 tells us that, *"Therefore to him that knoweth to do good, and doeth it not, to him it is sin."* This is impossible for an infant to acknowledge or experience. Then, Luther wants you to believe that God will condemn this infant, should it die, because the parents did not have it baptized!

❖ ***Infants Already Belong To The Kingdom of God.***

In Luke 18:15, infants were brought to Christ, along with little children. In Verse 16 Christ announces, *"...for **of such** is the kingdom of God."* Neither the little children, nor the infants, were ever baptized; yet, they belonged to the "kingdom of God." Since the Word of God is true, Luther would have to be labeled a liar and a deceiver.

❖ ***David's Son.***

Remember, again, King David's son, who died, being only seven days old. (II Samuel 12:18). He was never baptized; yet, David said in Chapter 12:23, *"I shall go to him, but he shall not return to me."* I am sure you recall the 23rd Psalm, written by David as the Holy Spirit instructed. The last verse states, *"And I (David) will dwell in the house of the Lord Forever."* Since King David is going to *"dwell with the LORD forever"* and *"will be going to be with"* his son; we would have to conclude that his son, upon departing this earth after seven days, had gone to be with the LORD. David's son was never baptized; but has been with the LORD for over 3,000 years.

- ***What The "Man On The Street" Thinks About Luther's Statement, "Infants, Too, Can Believe."***

Luther says that "**Infants, too, can believe**," in his *Small Catechism*, P. 174, #626, C. I did something just for my own curiosity. I asked many, many people if they thought an infant child could believe something you told it. They all thought I was "nuts" to ask such a stupid question! Here are a few of the answers I received.

"What is your point, Pard?" "I don't have time for this foolishness!" "Are you taking a survey or something? I am really not interested." "Are you serious? Everybody knows an infant can't believe." "That's the dumbest question I have ever been asked!"

One man in particular, after I had asked him the same question, responded by the following. He said, "I know you know the answer to your own question and so do I, as we *both* know infants cannot believe. I have a little girl 3 months old." He further stated that I had stimulated his curiosity as to *why* I would ask such a question.

I told him this is what Martin Luther teaches in his Catechisms. He wasn't a Lutheran; but had some friends who were. He told me that his Lutheran friends were intelligent and responsible people and he couldn't believe his friends could believe something this bizarre. I told him he could read Luther's own words for himself on Page 174 in the *Small Catechism*. He was the only person who showed any interest at all in my question.

For someone to believe that an infant is capable of understanding and believing something, transgresses any intelligence or common sense God has created them with. You may hold a bottle of milk out to an infant and he may believe you are about to give it to him and cry when, instead, you take it away. However, he has no faculties to deal with abstract concepts like "sin" or "belief." Luther, ***magnetizes*** his followers to believe the ***impossible*** when he says, "**Infants, too, can believe.**" He has well earned the title of the "Master of Deceit!"

- ***Infant Baptism Is A Promise of False Security.***

Luther's doctrine of infant baptism gives a false promise of security which is nothing more than a TRAP DOOR TO HELL! The parents who have their infant baptized are usually given a baptismal document confirming the act, with the date, time, name, and age of the infant. The parents are assured by the pastor, Grandpa and Grandma, Aunt Susie, and *all* the relatives that their baby is now a child of God and its baptism "works forgiveness of sins, delivers from death and the devil and gives eternal salvation..." (*Luther's Small Catechism*, P.174).

As the child grows older, he or she is continually reminded of the foregoing. The certificate is framed, placed on the wall, honored and reverenced as assurance that the child possesses eternal life. Many times the parents will give these certificates to the child when he establishes his own home.

In witnessing to many Lutherans, who were baptized as an infant, I have found only a few who will believe the Word of God and trust Jesus Christ as their personal Savior. The majority, by far, will believe their parents and family who followed their pastor; who followed Luther, and will believe his Catechism in lieu of the Bible. How sad and tragic this is!

The town I started a church in contains approximately 600 people. Many are related in one way or another. There is one Catholic church, a Methodist church, and two Lutheran churches of the same denomination (ELCA). All four set the same "Trap Door to Hell" of infant baptism, which is found nowhere in the Bible!

Most people acknowledge Billy Graham as one of the greatest and most respected of evangelists America has produced. Never have I heard or read where Rev. Graham ever projected infant baptism as a doctrine of the Bible.

- ***A Warning To Parents From God's Word.***

In conclusion, the ***worst thing*** a parent could do, is to have their baby baptized thinking that is going to secure their eternal home in Heaven. You have then become the ***mediator*** between God and your child, because you have convinced your child his baptism will give him eternal life. As the child matures, why should he need Jesus Christ as his Savior, when you, as his parents have assured him his baptism has saved him or her? This is how damnable the practice of infant baptism is. You have swung the "Trap Door to Hell" shut on your own child!

As we have previously shown, all infants and babies, should they die, go immediately to be with the Lord. Nowhere in God's Word will you ever find an infant being baptized. Nowhere will you read in the Bible that God ever ***instructs*** parents to baptize their babies. When a child reaches the age of accountability where they comprehend that God loves them and Jesus Christ paid for their sins on the cross; they are, then, responsible to accept or reject Christ's payment.

Peter stated very clearly in Acts 4:12, *"Neither is there salvation in any other:* (This includes Martin Luther and his pseudo-doctrine of infant baptism.) *for there is none other name under heaven given among men, whereby we must be saved."*

In John 3:36 is recorded a very simple truth concerning eternal life. *"He that believeth on the Son hath everlasting life: and he that believeth not the Son shall not see life; but the wrath of God abideth on him."*

Instructions to the head of the family are given in Ephesians 6:4. *"And, ye fathers, provoke not your children to wrath: but bring them up in the nurture and admonition of the Lord."* (Not Luther's "Catechism of Philosophy").

Parents, who will you believe? Martin Luther, the Master of Deceit with his "Trap Door to Hell" of infant baptism; OR, the *"**Savior**, which is Jesus Christ, the Lord,"* and eternal life. (Luke 1:11).

Jeremiah in 17:5 states God's advice.

> *"Thus saith the LORD; Cursed be the man that trusteth in man, and maketh flesh his arm, and whose heart departeth from the LORD."*

Chapter Five

Luther's False Doctrine of Baptismal Regeneration

- ***Introduction.***

Should there be any doubt in a person's mind that Luther was trusting in water baptism to give eternal life; his own words will substantiate his belief. On Page 16, #11, *Small Catechism*, he writes the following:

> **"THE BLESSINGS OF BAPTISM, What does baptism give or profit? It works forgiveness of sins, delivers from death and the devil, and gives eternal salvation to all who believe this..."**

Luther quotes the same on Page 174, #11, *Small Catechism.* On Page 177, #257, Luther explains the meaning of the above statements.

> **"The word of God places these great blessings into baptism; and through faith, which trusts this word of promise, we accept the forgiveness, life and SALVATION OFFERED IN BAPTISM and make these blessings our own."**

Luther further states on Page 179, last paragraph, *Small Catechism*, the following:

> **"By baptism we are made partakers of Christ."**

Here are some more of Luther's words concerning his faith in water baptism for salvation, as stated in his *Large Catechism*:

- Page 81, #6 - **"Moreover it is solemnly and strictly commanded that we must be baptized, or we shall NOT be saved."**

- Page 83, #24 - **"To put it most simply, the power, effect, benefit, fruit, and PURPOSE OF BAPTISM IS TO SAVE." To be saved, we know, is nothing else than to be delivered from sin, death, and the devil and to enter into the Kingdom of Christ and live with Him forever."**

- Page 85, #36 - **"But it becomes beneficial to you if you accept it as God's command and ordinance, so that, baptized in the name of God, you may receive *in the water, the promised salvation."***

- Page 86, #44 - **"But I am baptized! And if I am baptized, I have the promise that I shall be saved and have eternal life, both in soul and body."**

- Page 86, #46a - **"Since the water and the word together constitute one baptism, body and soul shall be saved and live forever."**

- Page 86, 46b - **"No greater jewel, therefore, can adorn our body and soul than baptism, for through it we obtain perfect holiness and salvation, which no other kind of life and no work on earth can acquire."**

I could go on and on in quoting Luther and his faith in baptism for Salvation.

- ***Luther Says, "Faith is Not Necessary for Baptism to be Valid."***

As I was studying *Luther's Large Catechism,* I read something I could hardly believe, so I went back and re-read it several times. Allow me to ask you a simple question. How many times have you heard preachers and laymen quote Luther as having said, "*The just shall live by faith?"* That is supposed to be one of his famous statements.

But, in his *Large Catechism*, he states that as long as you have been baptized, even though you do not have faith, it does not render your baptism for eternal life void. This is nothing more than Satanic heresy! Before I quote Luther, allow me to enlighten your knowledge as to the meaning of the word "heresy." The Greek is *"hairesis,"* as defined in *Vine's Expository Dictionary of Greek New Testament Words.*

> "An opinion, especially a self-willed opinion, which is substituted for submission to the power of truth, and leads to division and the formation of sects. Such erroneous opinions are frequently the outcome of personal preference of the prospect of advantage."

Here are Luther's words as stated in his *Large Catechism:*

- **"Further, we are not primarily concerned whether the baptized person believes or not, for in the latter case (i.e., does not believe) Baptism does NOT become invalid."** (Page 87, #52).

- **"Baptism is valid, even though faith be lacking." Baptism does not become invalid even if it is wrongly received or used, for it is bound NOT to our faith, but to the Word."** (Page 87, #53).

- **Even though a Jew should today come deceitfully and with an evil purpose, and we baptized him in all good faith, we should have to admit that his baptism was valid (i.e., gave him eternal life and etc.).** (Page 87, #54).

Re-read the definition of heresy in the above paragraph with a desire to know the truth about Luther and you would run from this man, the "Master of Deceit." God's Word exposes this man's philosophy as being fraudulent. Here is God's rebuke of Luther.

> *"Therefore being justified by faith, we have peace with God through our Lord Jesus Christ. By whom also we have access by faith into this grace wherein we stand, and rejoice in hope of the glory of God."* (Romans 5:1,2).

Notice Romans 4:3 concerning Abraham:

> *"For what saith the scripture? Abraham believed God, and it was counted unto him for righteousness."*

Since Martin Luther believes that Baptism gives one eternal life; then, you would have to conclude that Luther is saying you don't have to believe, or have faith to inherit eternal life! BUT, God disagrees! Let's see what God has to say about faith and being saved in Ephesians 2:8,9.

> *"For by grace are ye* ***saved through faith****; and that not of yourselves: it is the gift of God, Not of works, lest any man should boast."*

In James 2:8, God's Word states that, *"A double minded man is unstable in ALL his ways."* I am afraid Luther would be classified in this category. Luther states one thing in one place and contradicts himself in another, time after time.

Notice in *Luther's Small Catechism*, Page 177, #257, he states that,

> **"The word of God places these great blessings into baptism; and *through faith*, which trusts this word of promise, we accept the forgiveness, life, and salvation offered in baptism..."**

Here, Luther says you must have faith in baptism to receive the blessings. Now, in his *Large Catechism*, he says the opposite, therefore CONTRADICTING HIMSELF. Allow me to quote his words on Page 87, #52.

> **"Further, we are not primarily concerned whether the baptized person believes or**

> **not, for in the latter case, baptism does not become invalid."**

Then on Page 87, #53, he further reveals his thinking by stating that...

> **"Baptism is valid, even though faith be lacking."**

Luther is quoted as saying, "*The just shall live by faith,*" as the Word of God states in Romans 1:17; Galatians 3:11, etc. This statement by Luther is very deceiving as it leads one to believe, especially a born-again Christian, that Luther is trusting Jesus Christ and, ***him alone,*** for his salvation, the same as they have. Nothing could be further from the truth! Luther's statement that, "*The just shall live by faith,*" is meant as *faith in water baptism* for salvation, as he states over and over in his Catechisms.

Therefore, if you were to ask a Lutheran if they believed that Christ was crucified, buried and rose again as payment for their sins, they would almost exclusively answer, "Yes." From this response, the average Christian would assume that they were saved. But, such is not the case!

Luther believed, historically, that Christ died and rose again, making it possible for anyone to possess eternal life. But, Luther did not trust in, believe in, or have faith in, the ***finished work of Christ ALONE*** for salvation. In other words, he believed that Christ paid for our sins and would give eternal life on one condition. Even though Christ paid for our sins, the "switch" of water baptism is what gives us eternal life and makes us a child of God, according to Luther. Notice Luther's words.

> **"God's name was given to us when we became *Christians at Baptism,* and so we are called children of God."** (*Large Catechism*, Page 69, #37).

As usual, the Word of God is in sharp contrast to the words of Luther. Notice John 1:12.

> *"But as many as received him* (Christ), *to them gave he power to become the sons of God, even to them that believe on his name."*

Therefore, Luther's meaning concerning, "*The just shall live by faith,*" is *faith in baptism* which throws the "switch" of salvation to those who believe this. The biblical definition is, "Faith in Jesus Christ, plus nothing, for salvation;" **not**, faith in water baptism.

One must remember a follower of Luther *does* believe in the Trinity, the Bible as God's Word; and that Jesus Christ, by his death and resurrection, has provided salvation for the world. So far so good! This is what a Christian is trusting in for their salvation, "plus nothing!" Not so with Luther. He believed Christ only **purchased** salvation; but, would only give it to those who were baptized. That is "plus works," and will never result in eternal life.

- ***"Baptismal Water is Divine Water."***

In Ephesians 2:8,9 we are told...

> *"For by grace are ye saved through faith; and that not of yourselves: it is the gift of God. Not of works, lest any man should boast."*

The difference between a Christian and Luther, a religious man, is that Luther went beyond simple faith in Christ, believing salvation was not obtained or implemented until you were baptized. Since baptism is a work of the flesh, that of the baptizer and the baptized, Luther had to devise some scheme to get around the words *"not of works,"* found in Ephesians 2:8,9, and this he did.

Anyone that knows anything about the Word of God, knows that what is done in the flesh is a *work*; while believing, trust, faith, etc. is done with the *mind*!

Luther now sets out to convince his followers that baptism is not a work of the flesh and that the baptismal water becomes "DIVINE WATER" when his preachers pronounce the words, "baptizing them in the name of the Father, the Son and of the holy Ghost." It is at this time, Luther contends, that the "water is not just water;" but, now turns into "DIVINE WATER." Now, it is "saving water." Let us listen to the words of Luther, himself.

> **"It is not simply common water, but water comprehended in God's Word and commandment and sanctified by them. It is**

nothing else than a DIVINE WATER." (*Large Catechism*, Page 82, Par. #14).

"God himself stakes his honor, his power, and his might on it. Therefore it is not simply a natural water, but a DIVINE, HEAVENLY, HOLY, and BLESSED WATER."(*Large Catechism*,Page 82, Par. #17).

Now Luther, hopefully, with these words has convinced his followers that this water, with all of these godly adjectives attached, will now save you. Since the water has now been "activated," it now can save! Here are Luther's own words.

"To put it most simply, the power, effect, benefit, fruit, and purpose of baptism is to save." (*Large Catechism*, Page 83, Par. #24).

Now that Luther has the water purified, sanctified and "electrified," it can give eternal salvation! The only problem is, nowhere in the New Testament do you find "Divine Water," "Heavenly Water," "Holy Water," or "Blessed Water." Luther continually adds to God's Word what the Holy Spirit *forgot* to put in, which seems to be Luther's opinion!

- ***Luther Says that "Baptism is Not a Work."***

Luther now has one more hurdle to get over; and, that is, getting you to believe the act of baptism is not a work of the flesh. Remember Ephesians 2:8,9, God's Word, tells us that we are saved by FAITH. Salvation is a GIFT of God, and salvation is NOT OF WORKS!

> *"For by grace are ye saved through faith; and that not of yourselves: it is the gift of God: Not of works, lest any man should boast."* (Ephesians 2:8-9).

In Ephesians 2:9 we find the word "work" is translated from the Greek word "*ergon*," and is a noun, "(from a primary but obsolete root "ergo, or "to work") and means "to toil as an effort or occupation; by implication, an act, deed, doing, labour, work." (*Strong's Exhaustive Concordance of the Bible).*

The Book of James makes a distinction between the works of the flesh and faith, which comes from our mind by *thinking*!

> *"Yea, a man may say, Thou hast faith, and I have works: Shew me thy faith without thy works, and I will shew thee my faith by my works."*

Here one can easily see that faith is of the mind, ***internally,*** and works of the flesh are expressed ***externally!*** Romans 4:5 also makes the distinction between works and faith/belief (synonymous terms).

> *"But to him that worketh not, but believeth on him that justifieth the ungodly, his faith is counted for righteousness."* (Romans 4:5).

The flesh can produce good works or bad works. Our legs can take one to church, or take one to a brothel.

Our arms can embrace someone out of love, or hit someone out of anger. Our mouth can praise someone out of love, or gossip about someone out of hate, etc.

When a person is baptized, they bring their ***body*** to be baptized. They don't send their spirit to be baptized, while their body stays at home! When a person is baptized, the flesh brought them, whether they walked, drove, or were carried to the location. The preacher used his hand to dip in the water and sprinkle some on the head of the baptized.. These are all accomplished by the works of the flesh.

Now, according to God's Word, any act done with the body is a work of the flesh. But, Luther has to convince you that baptism is not a work, or it would contradict all other Scriptures that exclude good works for salvation. Here is Luther's philosophy, which is found nowhere in the Bible.

> **"*Baptism is not a work which we do* but is a treasure which God gives and faith grasps, just as the Lord *Christ upon the cross is not a work*, but a treasure comprehended and offered to us in the word and received by faith."** (*Large Catechism*, Page 85, Par. #37).

The following words from Luther are unbelievable and, not only a lie; but an *insult* to the normal intelligence of a human being. This is what every cult leader has to do in order to promote their philosophy in perverting the Word of God.

> **"To be baptized in God's name is to be baptized *not by men* but by God Himself. Although it is performed by men's hands, it is nevertheless truly God's own act."** (*Large Catechism*, Page 81, Par.#10).

It seems to me that when the followers of Luther read the Catechism, they accept his words as though they were the Bible, itself. I have found this, personally, to be true in my conversations with hundreds of Lutherans.

To stimulate your thinking, let us compare Luther's words with God's Word.

- ***Luther:*** **"Baptism is not a work which we do."**

  The Bible: Cannot be found in the Bible because it is not true!

  Conclusion: Luther lied to deceive you.

- ***Luther***: **"Christ upon the cross is not a work."**

  The Bible: Cannot be found in the Bible.

  Conclusion: Luther lied again to deceive.

- ***Luther***: **"Baptism is a treasure which God gives."**

  The Bible: Nowhere did God ever associate the word "treasure" with baptism.

Conclusion – Luther lied again to deceive, by adding to the Word of God.

***Luther*: "To be baptized in God's name is *not* to be baptized by men, but by God Himself."**

***Luther*: "Although it (baptism) is performed by men's hands, it is nevertheless God's own act."**

The Bible: Nowhere can you find these words of Luther in the Bible.

Conclusion: Luther wants me to believe that men do the baptizing; but, it is not really them. It is God, Himself, who is really doing the baptizing.

Since Christ is God manifested in the flesh, why has no one ever seen Christ, in His Person, baptizing anyone down here? I have baptized, by submersion, scores of believers in over 35 years of ministry. I never had the Lord step in and say, "I will take over from here and do the baptizing.

You are probably thinking, "This is the craziest thing I have ever heard anyone say!" I most assuredly agree with you! It is not only crazy; but, the thinking of an unsaved man trying, by his natural mind to adjust the Scriptures to his own preconceived theology, which he inherited from the Roman Catholic organization.

The conclusion to the previous statements by Luther, as they are given above, is nothing more than a lie to magnetize your thinking into believing that God, Himself, actually baptized you, and now you are saved!

- ***Summary.***

You may be wondering how and why a religious man like Luther will not trust Jesus Christ and Him ALONE for his salvation?

> *"He that believeth on the Son hath everlasting life: and he that believeth not the Son shall not see life; but the wrath of God abideth on him."* (John 3:36).

You will find, in the Word of God, that not one person was ever water baptized to be saved. All of those that were baptized were already believers.

Luther, like every other cult leader, DENIES that Salvation, i.e., eternal life is only obtained by faith in Jesus Christ, and faith alone. The ***reason*** these false teachers do not believe this is clearly explained in I Corinthians.

> *"But the natural* (i.e., lost) *man receiveth not the things of the Spirit of God: for they are foolishness unto him: neither can he know them, because they are spiritually discerned."* (I Corinthians 2:14).

I hope by this time you have an opened and keen mind to see the cleverness, adroitness, and skillfulness of Luther. I hope you can see how he constantly has one Scripture contradicting another in order to embrace his philosophy of baptismal regeneration.

Remember, Friend, the difference between Luther's salvation by baptism and God's salvation through Christ, is where you are going to spend Eternity. If you believe Martin Luther, it is Hell. If you believe the Bible, God's Word, it is Heaven. The Bible says,

> *"It is better to trust in the LORD than to put confidence in man."* (Psalm 118:8).

Baptismal regeneration is Satan's "Trap Door to Hell," believed by, and perpetrated upon, countless numbers of unsuspecting followers by the "Master of Deceit," Martin Luther.

Chapter Six

Luther's Skill In Deception Regarding Baptismal Regeneration

In this Chapter we are going to examine a method of deception used by Luther to endorse his false doctrine of baptismal regeneration. This is a sly, cunning procedure whereby he makes a statement, and then *appears* to back it up from the Bible. He does not *actually* back up his statement from the Bible; but, simply gives you the reference and does not quote the verses. If you take the time to read the Bible verses which you *think* are proving Luther's point, you will find that Luther is actually contradicting the Word of God. He just hoped you would not take the time to read the verses!

The verses used by Luther to endorse his false doctrine of baptismal regeneration are the same verses used by the Roman Catholic organization and the Church of Christ. All three believe that baptism saves you.

- ***Some Basic Principles of Biblical Interpretation***

When studying the Word of God, there are basic principles which must be followed in order to obtain the proper understanding of a particular verse or passage. The Lord lets us know in II Timothy 3:16 that,

> *"All Scripture is given by inspiration of God, and is profitable for doctrine, for reproof, for correction, for instruction in righteousness."*

Also, concerning the inspiration of Scripture, we are instructed as to the use of Scripture in II Peter 1:20.

> *"Knowing this first, that no prophesy of the scripture is of an private interpretation."*

In II Timothy 3:16, the word "*inspiration*," as all Bible students know, means "God-breathed." In other words, God breathed into the minds of the writers of Scripture exactly what He wanted them to write. We know that the God of Creation is Omnipotent, i.e., all powerful. He is also Omniscient, i.e., all knowing; as well as Omnisapience, or all wisdom. These attributes assure us that the Scriptures, as *originally penned*, are without error or contradiction.

Anyone can make, dishonestly, the Bible to mean whatever they want it to. For example: the Bible says in Psalm 14:1 that *"...There is no God."* But, that is only taking part of the verse. The whole verse reads,*" The fool hath said in his heart, There is no God. They are corrupt, that have done abominable works, there is none that doeth good.*" The Bible further tells us that, *"Every word of God is pure."* (Proverbs 30:5).

Therefore, in studying the Bible it is important to apply some very simple principles to keep from falling into believing a false doctrine. It is not my intention to go into a full discourse on Inspiration, Illumination, and Interpretation at this time. My purpose is to keep it simple, so the man, woman, boy or girl on the street can understand.

The following are the ***four simple principles*** that must be followed:

1. ***Never add to or take away from the Scriptures.*** Proverbs 30:6, *"Add thou not unto his words, lest he reprove thee, and thou be found a liar."*

2. ***Never take part of a verse or text out of its context.*** By "context," we mean the surrounding verses. By doing so, you will not only deceive yourself, but those that follow you. Luther was a master at this, as we shall see.

3. ***Never build a doctrine where one verse seemingly contradicts another verse.***

4. ***Never accept the translation of a word that contradicts a Biblical doctrine or principle.*** Go to your Strong's Concordance and see if the word has been mistranslated. One must remember that the original writers were inspired of God; therefore the original manuscripts were without error. The King James Translation from the Hebrew and Greek into the English is, by far, superior to any translation we have today; although the translators were not inspired, as were the original writers. Therefore, if a word or verse seems to contradict Scripture, then we must check to see if a translational error is the cause.

Allow me to give you a very simple illustration of what I mean from the Bible. We know, as a Christian, that we still have the old nature and are capable of sinning, even after we are saved. I John 1:8 makes this perfectly clear.

> *"If we say, that we have no sin, we deceive ourselves, and the truth is not in us."*

But in Galatians 5:17, we find a verse that tells us that we, as Christians CANNOT do the things that our sinful flesh wants us to do.

> *"For the flesh lusteth against the Spirit, and the Spirit against the flesh: and these are contrary the one to the other: so that ye cannot do the things that ye would."*

Here we seem to have a problem, as Galatians 5:17 says that we ***cannot*** do the sins that the flesh wants us to. Then I John tells me in 1:8 that, *If I say I have no sin, I have deceived myself..."*

How do we reconcile these two verses that seem to be in direct conflict with each other? The first place we go is to our concordance and look up the word *"cannot"* and see if it is properly translated from the Greek. Here we find the Greek for *"cannot"* is *"me"* pronounced "may" and is not in the absolute sense; but is a prime particle of qualified negation and should be translated "should not, or may not."

There is another Greek word *"ouch,"* translated *"cannot,"* which is in the absolute sense. This appears in I Corinthians 15:50,

> *"Now this I say, brethren, that flesh and blood cannot* (Greek *"ouch") inherit the kingdom of God."*

How easily this so-called contradiction is eradicated by checking the translation of one word in the concordance.

Now may I draw your attention to Principle Number One, ***"Neither add to or take away from the***

Scripture." Since Luther preaches, teaches and is trusting baptism for his salvation, it amazes me, how deceitful and clever this man is in order to convince you he is right. Follow with me as we discover ***Luther's scheme of taking away and adding to,*** God's Word. The following is emphasized and his words are shown here as they appear in his *Small Catechism* on Page 172.

> **"250. What distinction is to be made in baptizing?**
>
> **A. Those who can receive instruction are to be baptized after they have been *instructed* in the *principle doctrines* of the Christian religion. 621. They that gladly received his word were baptized. Acts 2:41.**
>
> **Bible Narratives:**
>
> **The Ethiopian was *instructed* before he was baptized. Acts 8:26-39.**
>
> **The jailer was *instructed* before he was baptized. Acts 16:25-33."**

❖ ***The First Error is Luther's "Principle Doctrine"***

The first, and most interesting, statement that Luther makes here is that you must be "***instructed*** in the ***principle doctrines*** of the Christian religion" before you are baptized. A Christian, reading this, would naturally assume that Luther was instructing the person in the Scriptures concerning salvation; so they would have the assurance of eternal life by trusting Jesus Christ as their personal Savior. Therefore, he would *surely* use such verses such as John 3:15-18; John 5:24; John 11:25,26; or John 3:36, which is here quoted:

> *"He that believeth on the Son hath everlasting life: and he that believeth not the Son shall not see life; but the wrath of God abideth on him."*

Now, let us listen to Luther, himself, as he clarifies what he means by the ***"principle doctrines of the Christian religion."*** Remember, Luther ***does not*** believe that faith in Jesus Christ, alone, gives you eternal life! Eternal life, i.e., salvation, is not obtained until you are baptized. The following, you will take notice, does not contain the Biblical Doctrine of Soteriology (i.e., the Doctrine of Salvation). The following is recorded in *Luther's Small Catechism*, P.39, Paragraphs 4,5.

"4. What does Luther's Small Catechism contain?

Luther's Small Catechism contains *the chief parts of the Christian Doctrine."*

5. Which are the chief parts of Christian doctrine?

1. The Ten Commandments.
2. The Apostles' Creed
3. The Lord's Prayer
4. The Sacrament of Holy Baptism

5. The Office of the Keys and Confession
6. The Sacrament of the Altar"

This is what Luther instructs a person about before they are to be baptized. Now that Luther has instructed the person in the above six principles, they are ready to receive their baptism; or, Number 4., as Luther puts it, "The Sacrament of Holy Baptism." Nowhere does God ever use the word "holy" with the word "baptism" in the Bible. This is just another ***adding to the Word of God*** by Luther's philosophy.

On Page 174, #II, in *Luther's Small Catechism*, he tells us what he ***instructs*** a person ***about*** concerning their baptism.

> **"What does Baptism give or profit? It works forgiveness of sins, delivers from death and the devil, and gives eternal salvation to all who believe this..."**

❖ ***The Second Error – The Ethiopian Eunuch.***

Let us continue to examine Luther's words as stated on Page 172, Par. 250, in his *Small Catechism*. I want you to notice carefully in these two paragraphs of Luther's narrative where he very cunningly and skillfully uses the word "INSTRUCTED" three different times. We have just covered its use in the first paragraph; i.e., that his baptism would save him. Now, in the last paragraph, he uses two illustrations to mislead you into thinking that baptism will save you.

In order to do this concerning the *Ethiopian Eunuch*, as recorded in Acts 8:26-39; and the *Philippian Jailer*, as recorded in Acts 16:25-33; he must keep you from acknowledging that both of these men were ***already saved***, before they were baptized. Luther very cleverly avoids *quoting* these two passages from the Word of God and simply gives the references where the verses can be found. He then devises his own rhetoric to magnetize your thinking to agree with him. Luther states that:

> **"The Ethiopian was INSTRUCTED before he was baptized. Acts 8:26-39."**
>
> **"The jailer was INSTRUCTED before he was baptized. Acts 16:25-33."**

If Luther had shown, from the context of these verses, that the Ethiopian Eunuch had already believed that Jesus Christ had previously died, was buried and had been resurrected to pay for his sin, and was already saved; then, Luther's baptismal salvation would have been proven a Satanic lie. Luther did not want you to know that.

Now, let's examine the Bible and see the truth. Phillip was directed by God (Acts 8:26-30) to witness to this Ethiopian Eunuch, and this he did. Phillip had found the Ethiopian sitting by the side of the road in a chariot, reading out of Isaiah 53:7,8. (Acts 8:31-33). In Verse 34, the Eunuch told Phillip that he didn't understand who Isaiah was speaking about. The explanation is found in Verse 35.

> *"Then Phillip opened his mouth, and began at the same scripture and preached unto him Jesus."*(Acts 8:35).

Any Bible student knows that the whole chapter of Isaiah 53 is prophetic of what Christ would fulfill 700 years later. Phillip showed the Eunuch what Christ had done to pay for our sins, as prophesied in Isaiah 53:5,6. Here is the record.

> *"But he* (Christ) *was wounded for our transgressions, he was bruised for our iniquities: the chastisement of our peace was upon him* (Christ)*; and with his stripes we are healed."*(V.5).

> *"All we like sheep have gone astray; we have turned everyone to his own way; and the LORD hath laid on him* (Christ) *the iniquity of us all."* (V.6).

We *know* the Eunuch *believed the Scriptures*, that Christ was crucified, buried, and risen again, as payment for his sin. Therefore, he was saved by believing what the Scriptures testify to, as John 6:47 states very simply,

> *"Verily, Verily, I* (Christ) *say unto you, He that believeth on me hath everlasting life."*

We, also, know the Ethiopian Eunuch was *saved* before he was baptized, because he said he believed,

> *"And he* (the Ethiopian Eunuch) *answered and said, I believe that Jesus Christ is the Son of God."*
>
> *(Acts 8:37b).*

This is what Luther does not want you to believe. This is why he didn't quote the Bible; but, instead, gave you his own philosophy in stating,

> **"The Ethiopian was INSTRUCTED before he was baptized."**

If Luther really believed the Bible, he would have told his followers the truth by stating,

> **"The Ethiopian was SAVED before he was baptized."**

Nowhere in the Bible do you ever find anyone being baptized who was not already saved. Philip would not have baptized the Eunuch, unless he had confirmation that he was saved. The record is perfectly clear as stated in Acts 8:36-38. We shall quote it in its entirety.

> *"And the Eunuch said, See, here is water; What doth hinder me to be baptized?"* (V.36).

> *"And Philip said, If thou* <u>*believest*</u> *with all thine heart* (i.e., no reservations whatsoever), *thou mayest. And he answered and said, I* <u>*believe*</u> *that Jesus Christ is the Son of God."* (V.37).

> *"And he commanded the chariot to stand still: and they went down both into the water, both Philip and the Eunuch; and he baptized him."* (V.38).

The Ethiopian Eunuch was baptized ***after*** believing in Jesus Christ for his salvation.

❖ *The Third Error. – The Philippian Jailer*

In referring back to *Luther's Small Catechism*, Page 172, Par. 250, we find his third error in an attempt to deceive people into believing that baptism saves you. He does this very cleverly by inserting his word "instructed" instead of God's word "saved."

Here are Luther's words,

> **"The jailer was "instructed" before he was baptized." Acts 16:25-33.**

We shall not rehearse what has already been covered in *"The Second Error"*, previously; what Luther means by "being instructed." Luther was smart enough NOT to quote the Bible in Acts 16:25-33, which clearly states that the jailer was saved by believing in Christ ***before*** he was baptized. This, of course, would contradict Luther's claim that you are not saved until after you ARE baptized!

Perhaps he got away with this at the time of writing his *Small Catechism* because most common folks couldn't read well, or didn't have a Bible anyway! And most modern folks don't bother to check the Scripture as their attitude is, "If Luther said it, I believe it!"

Therefore, reading the Catechism and being a Lutheran, you would naturally assume that the jailer was being ***instructed*** as to the benefit and profit of being baptized. Here are Luther's own words in his *Small Catechism,* P.16, under "II. The Blessings of Baptism."

> **What does Baptism give or profit? It works forgiveness of sins, delivers from death and the devil, and gives eternal salvation to all who believe this..."**

Now, if Luther had stated the truth that, "The jailer was SAVED, instead of INSTRUCTED, before he was baptized;" then, the Scriptures would have exposed Luther as a false teacher and a liar in his Catechism on P.16 under "II. The Blessings of Baptism."

Let us examine the Scripture references he gives; ***but, does not quote***, in the hope that you will not go to the Bible and read it for yourself.

Acts 16:25-33. Paul and Silas were arrested for their preaching in Philippi. They were beaten (V.22,23); thrown into prison and their feet chained (V.24). While in this prison, they prayed and sang praises unto God (V.25). God sent a great earthquake which caused the doors to unlock and their chains to be loosed. (V. 26). It woke up the jailer, who saw the doors opened and thought the prisoners had escaped and was about to kill himself. (V.27). Paul yelled to him that everybody was still here. (Vs. 28,29). The jailer was trembling; or, as we would say, scared to death! A jailer who lost his prisoners was usually killed. (See Acts 12:19).

Then the jailer asked Paul and Silas that famous question, *"What must I do to be saved?"* (V.30). Their answer was NOT as Luther would have told him, i.e., "Ye must be baptized to be saved." Instead, Paul and Silas told him the truth, *"**Believe** on the Lord Jesus Christ, and thou shalt be saved, and thy house."* (V.31).

Notice Acts 16:32.

> *"And they spake unto him the word of the Lord, and to ALL that were in his house."*

The jailer took Paul and Silas to his home where they told his whole family how to be saved. The "*word of the Lord*" would have been what Jesus said. In John 14:6, we are told,

> *"Jesus saith unto him, I am the way, the truth and the life: no man cometh unto the Father, but by me."*

Paul preached faith in Christ for salvation wherever he went, and NEVER baptism for salvation! In fact, when writing to the Corinthians, he made it perfectly clear that baptism was NOT the Gospel!

> *"For Christ sent me not to baptize, BUT to preach the gospel: not with wisdom of words, lest the cross of Christ should be made of none effect."* (I Corinthians 1:17).

Now, back to the jailer and his family in Acts 16:34, where we read...

> *"And when he had brought them into his house, he set meat before them, and rejoiced, believing in God with ALL his house."*

What does it mean, "The whole family "believed in God?" They simply believed what Christ said in John 3:16.

> *"For God so loved the world, that he gave his only begotten Son, that whosoever believeth in him should not perish, but have everlasting life."*

> *"And this is the record, that God hath given to us eternal life, and this life is in his Son.* (Not in baptism!)" (I John 5:11).

After the jailer and his family were saved by hearing and believing the truth from Paul and Silas, as stated in Acts 16:31,

> *"And they said, Believe on the Lord Jesus Christ, and thou shalt be saved, and thy house."*

Then they were baptized ***after*** they were saved, NOT as a condition ***to be saved***, as recorded in Verse 34.

> *"And he took them the same hour of the night, and washed their stripes* (wounds); *and was baptized, he* (the jailer) *and all his house* (the whole family). (Acts 16:34).

The foregoing is only a brief example; or "the tip of the iceberg." It reveals how sly and cunning Luther really is, by inserting his philosophy to deceive the people into believing his damnable doctrine of baptismal regeneration.

One must never forget that, in 1508 at the age of 25, Luther was appointed to a University in Wittenberg, Germany, as a public teacher of Philosophy. God's warning against such men as Luther is found in Colossians 2:8.

"Beware lest any man spoil you through philosophy and vain deceit, after the tradition of men, and the rudiments of the world, and not after Christ."

- ***Fourth Error – Luther Places His Catechism Above God's Word.***

Luther contends for your time and faith, to read and study his Catechism and to believe his writings. Allow me to qualify this statement by Luther's own words as stated in his *Large Catechism* following the heading, **"MARTIN LUTHER'S PREFACE."**

1. **"It is not for trivial reasons that we constantly treat the *Catechism* and strongly urge others to do the same."** (P.2, Par.1).

2. **"Yet I do as a child who is being taught the *Catechism.*"** (P.3, Par 7).

3. **"I must still read and study the *Catechism* daily, yet I cannot master it as I wish, but must remain a child and pupil of the *Catechism.*"** (P.3, Par. 8).

4. **"Even if their knowledge of the *Catechism* were perfect (though that is not possible in this life), yet it is highly profitable and fruitful daily to read it (the Catechism) and make it the subject of meditation and conversation."** (P.3, Par. 9).

5. **"So that day by day we relish and appreciate the *Catechism.*"** (P.3, Par. 9).

6. **"For this reason alone you should eagerly read, recite, ponder, and practice the *Catechism*."**(P.4, Par. 11).

7. **"If this were not enough to admonish us to read the *Catechism* daily, there is God's command."** (P.4, Par. 11). (I am not aware of *any* verse in the Bible which commands us we should read *either* of Luther's Catechisms! This is an outright lie!)

8. **"Look at those bored, presumptuous saints who will not or cannot read and study the *Catechism* daily."** (P.5, Par. 16).

9. **"Let all Christians exercise themselves in the *Catechism* daily, and constantly put it into practice."** (P.5, Par. 19).

10. **"This sermon has been undertaken for the instruction of children and uneducated people. Hence from ancient times it has been called in Greek, a "*Catechism*" – that is, instruction for children. Whoever does not possess it (the *Catechism*) should not be reckoned among Christians nor admitted to a sacrament."** (P.6, Par.1,2).

11. **"For this reason young people should be thoroughly instructed in the various parts of the *Catechism* or children's sermons and diligently drilled in their practice."** (P.6, Par. 3).

Should one claim to be a Lutheran, then you are sending a message that you believe in Luther's writings in his Catechisms, his philosophy, and his doctrine of salvation by baptism. Looking at #6, above, one can easily see that Luther wants to indoctrinate your thinking with his philosophy as set forth in his Catechism. Here are his words.

> **"...You should eagerly read, recite, ponder and practice the Catechism."**

Christ refutes Luther and every other false teacher who directs you away from the Word of God and towards their writings. Here is what Christ has to say.

> *"But he* (Christ) *answered and said, It is written, Man shall not live by bread alone, but by every word that proceedeth out of the mouth of God."* (Matthew 4:4).

Notice carefully that Christ said, *"every word... out of the mouth of God"* (the Bible), NOT out of the mouth of Luther (the Catechism)

.

My purpose in putting in this section was to demonstrate the skill, craftiness, and cleverness of Martin Luther as he goes about deceiving millions into eternal damnation. Remember, Luther states over and over again in his Catechism that water baptism is what gives you eternal life. The Catechism is to Lutherans what the Bible is to Christians.

In our next section we will examine the verses Luther refers to in endorsing his damnable doctrine of baptismal regeneration.

> *"It is better to trust in the Lord than to put confidence in man."* (Psalm 118:8).

It is your choice as to who you want to believe. Luther's Catechism and the "Trap Door to Hell;" or, God's Word, the Bible, an open door to Heaven.

Chapter Seven

Luther's List of "Sugar Stick" Verses He Uses to Prove His False Doctrine of Baptismal Regeneration

In the ministry, an evangelist may have a few, favorite sermons in his, for lack of a better word, repertoire. These are sometimes jokingly referred to as "Sugar Stick" sermons. However, it is no joke when we review Martin Luther's favorite teachings! The following is a list of verses that Luther and his followers are trusting which they hope will prove that baptism is the way to have salvation.

- **Luther's First "Sugar Stick" is I Corinthians 6:11**:

(As Quoted by Martin Luther in His *Small Catechism*, P.176, Par. 636).

> **"(And such were some of you:) but ye are *washed*, but ye are *sanctified*, but ye are justified in the name of the Lord Jesus, and *by the Spirit of our God*."** (The words in parentheses are omitted in the Catechism.)

Nowhere in this verse does the word "baptism" appear. Luther, in his *Small Catechism*, tells you to believe that *"washed"* means water baptism. We find a basic principle in II Peter 1:20, that must be followed to honestly evaluate Scripture correctly.

> *"Knowing this first, that no prophecy of the scripture is of any private interpretation."*

In other words, a person cannot take a verse of Scripture out of context and apply it to substantiate a preconceived doctrine, or idea. All Scriptures must agree with each other; or, one would have to conclude that God contradicted Himself, which is an impossibility. The contradiction would have to be in the man's ideas, not in God's Word. Paul verifies this as he states in I Corinthians 1:25.

> *"Because the foolishness of God is wiser than men; and the weakness of God is stronger than men."*

Let us compare Luther's interpretation that "washed" means "baptized for salvation" against the Word of God.

- The Apostle John disagrees with Luther in Revelation 1:5,

  "And from Jesus Christ, who is the faithful witness, and the first begotten of the dead, and the prince of the kings of the earth. Unto him that loved us, and washed us from our sins in his own blood,"(No baptism here!)

- The Apostle Peter disagrees with Luther – I Peter 1:18,19,

  "Forasmuch as ye know that ye were not redeemed with corruptible things, as silver and gold, from your vain conversation (Gr. "behavior") *received by tradition from your fathers;* (V.18).

  But with the precious blood of Christ, as of a lamb without blemish and without spot:" (No baptism here.)

- ❖ Also, Peter testifying to Cornelius, said in Acts 10:43,

  "To him (Christ) *give all the prophets witness, that through his name whosoever believeth in him shall receive remission of sins."*(No baptism here.)

- ❖ The Apostle Paul rebukes Luther's false doctrine of "salvation by baptism" time after time.

  "But to him that worketh not, but believeth on him that justifieth the ungodly, his faith is counted for righteousness." (Romans 4:5). (No baptism here.)

  "Therefore being justified by faith, we have peace with God through our Lord Jesus Christ:" (Romans 5:1). (No baptism here.)

- ❖ Isaiah's great prophecy in Isaiah 53:5 tells of our Salvation through Jesus Christ and Him alone.

  "But he (Christ) *was wounded for our transgressions, he was bruised for our iniquities: the chastisement of our peace was upon him; and with his stripes we are healed* (i.e.,saved)." (No baptism here!)

Luther is trusting his baptism for eternal life and wants you to do the same. Re-read the verses listed above and you will see how God's Word contradicts Luther's philosophy of baptismal regeneration. Always remember, that all Scriptures must agree; or the contradiction is that of the false teacher, NOT GOD! It always comes down to this,

"Who are you going to believe, God, or man?" As Romans 3:4 states,

> *"God forbid: yea, let God be true, but every man a liar..."*

- **Luther's Second "Sugar Stick" is Acts 2:38:**

> **"Repent, and *be baptized* every one of you in the name of Jesus Christ *for the remission of sins."*** (*Luther's Small Catechism*, P.175, Par.629).

This is one of Luther's "sugar sticks" that he relies upon to support his "salvation by baptism." To erase any doubt that Luther's faith is in his baptism for the remission of sins, may I quote his words preceding Acts 2:38 in his Catechism.

> **"253. What great things, then, does baptism give or work? A. It works *forgiveness of sins.*"**

Acts 2:38 is a classic example of how "one little word" can change the whole meaning of a verse. The key to the proper understanding of this verse is found in the little Greek word "EIS," translated "*for*." The Greek word "EIS" is translated various ways in the New Testament, depending on the context and the usage of the word itself, by demonstrating BASIS, GROUND, AIM, or PURPOSE.

For example, in Matthew 12:41, "EIS" is translated "at," demonstrating the basis, or grounds. The preaching of

Jonah was the ***grounds*** for the repentance of Nineveh. *"...because they repented at* (Gr. "EIS" or "because of") *the preaching of Jonas."*

A.T. ROBERTSON, a well-known Greek scholar has pointed out that the Greek preposition, "EIS," translated "for" in the phrase, "for the remission of sins," may also mean "because of." An example of this can be found in Luke 11:32, where the text says that the people of Nineveh, *"...repented **at** the preaching of Jonas..."* The word "at" is a translation of the same Greek term "EIS" found in Acts 2:38. The people of Jonah's day, you see, did not repent FOR his preaching; but, BECAUSE of it."

DR. JOHN R. RICE, the founder of the *"Sword of The Lord"* newspaper, and a prolific writer who has authored volumes of books on the Bible, and is a worthy scholar known world-wide, agrees with this translation of "EIS." In one of his books entitled, *"Filled With The Spirit, The Book of Acts, A Verse-by-Verse Commentary*, he states the following in his exposition of Acts 2:38:

"The King James translation of Acts 2:38, '...be baptized everyone of you in the name of Jesus Christ *for* the remission of sins...' is unfortunate and inaccurate. The little Greek preposition, *EIS*, translated *for*, is an indefinite preposition of reference. It does not mean *in order to* receive the remission of sins, or he would have needed to use the Greek preposition *HINA*, which means *in order to*. He did not.

Even in English the preposition for does not necessarily mean, *in order to.* Often *for* means 'on the basis of,' or 'on the ground of.' Thus one is scolded *for* being late, or arrested *for* stealing, or praised *for* beauty, or rewarded *for* bravery, or paid *for* work. In that sense, only, is one baptized *for* remission of sins already obtained when one repented."

Therefore, in Acts 2:38, "*EIS*" is showing the "basis or grounds" for baptism; that of their "*remission of sins*" and "BECAUSE OF" their belief in Jesus Christ as their Savior. This would then be in perfect agreement with all other Scriptures concerning salvation.

Here is how the verse should literally be read in its proper translation:

> *"Then Peter said unto them, Repent* (Change your mind.)*, and be baptized every one of you in the name of Jesus Christ BECAUSE OF (Gr. "EIS") the remission of sins..."*

In other words, *"repent"* (Gr. "*metanoeō*," i.e. "change your mind") about Christ whom you crucified with wicked hands ("*hands of unbelief,*" Acts 2:23) and receive Him as your Savior. *Then,* be baptized; therefore, publicly identifying yourself with Him by the profession of your faith.

Acts 2:38 does not give a "new plan of salvation." It would be *contradictory* of Peter to proclaim salvation in Christ only; then state, "You have to be baptized to be saved. The Apostle Peter makes it very clear in Acts 4:12.

> *"Neither is there salvation in any other: for there is none other name under heaven given among men, whereby we must be saved."* (No baptism here!)

Peter, under the direction of the Holy Spirit, did not contradict himself, *or God*, in Acts 2:38. Here is a case in point where one little preposition, *"EIS,"* mistranslated, could change the meaning of the whole verse. This mistranslation is the villain which has caused this verse to *appear* to disagree with all other verses concerning salvation, which it does not.

- Peter gives a further testimony in Acts 15:9, at the Jerusalem Council, that Salvation is by FAITH, not baptism.

> *"And put no difference between us* (Jews) *and them* (Gentiles), *purifying their hearts by faith."* (No baptism here!)

- This is in perfect agreement with Romans 5:1.

> *"Therefore being justified by faith, we have peace with God through our Lord Jesus Christ:"* (Not baptism.)

God's word in Romans 6:23 states unequivocally that eternal life was bought and paid for by the death of Christ on the cross. It is thus offered as a free gift to anyone who will accept it by faith.

> *"For the wages of sin is death; but the GIFT of God is eternal life through Jesus Christ our Lord."* (Not baptism.)

Everyone knows that a gift is bought and paid for by someone else. The gift is purchased because of their love for the person they wish to give it to. This is exactly what God did because of His love for His creation, as described in John 3:16.

> *"For God so loved the world, that he gave his only begotten Son, that whosoever believeth in him* (Christ) *should not perish, but have everlasting life."* (No baptism here.)

Martin Luther *refuses* to accept salvation as a free gift by faith in Jesus Christ and Him ALONE. Here are Luther's words in his own Catechism. (*Large Catechism*, P. 86, Par. 44).

> **"But I am baptized! And if I am baptized, I have the promise that I shall be saved and have eternal life, both in soul and body."**

He then deletes 8 words out of a verse containing 17 words, in Mark 16:16, which leads us to...

- **Luther's Third "Sugar Stick" is Mark 16:16:**

> ***"He that believeth and is baptized shall be saved;(but he that believeth not shall be damned.)"*** (*Small Catechism*, P.175, Par. 633).

As is the custom of Luther, he again quotes only a part of a verse which he tries to use to support his line of thinking. Only what is not contained in the parentheses appears in his Catechism. The rest of the verse, shown in parenthesis, he omitted.

At one's first reading, "*He that believeth and is baptized shall be saved*" would seem contradictory to the multiplicity of verses which say we are saved by believing only.

- ❖ For example, I John 5:13 states authoritatively that a person can know with absolute certainty that they possess eternal life, yet there is no mention of water baptism.

  "These things have I written unto you that believe on the name of the Son of God; that ye may know that ye have eternal life, and that ye may believe on the name of the Son of God."

- ❖ Peter states it is not water baptism; or any human effort that redeems a person; but only the blood of Christ.

  "Forasmuch as ye know that ye were not redeemed with corruptible things, as silver and gold, from your vain conversation received by tradition from your fathers; (V.18).

But with the precious blood of Christ, as of a lamb without blemish and without spot:" (I Peter 1:18,19) (No baptism here!)

- And we find in John's Gospel,

"He that believeth on the Son hath everlasting life: and he that believeth not the Son shall not see life; but the wrath of God abideth on him." (John 3:36).

"Verily, verily, I say unto you, He that believeth on me hath everlasting life." (John 6:47).

Comparing these verses with Mark 16:16, there either has to be an explanation; or, we definitely have a contradiction between Peter, Mark and John! May I draw your attention to the last phrase in Mark 16:16, which Luther omitted in his *Small Catechism*, P. 175, Par. 633.

"...He that believeth not shall be damned..."

It does ***not*** say,

"...He that believeth not (and is not baptized) *shall be damned..."*

Only those who "*believe not*" shall be damned, which is in perfect accordance with John's statement in John 3:18,

"He that believeth on him is not condemned: but he that believeth not is condemned already, because he

> *hath not believed in the name of the only begotten Son of God."*

Both Mark 16:16 and John 3:18 state that a person is condemned if they do not believe; but *nothing* is said about being condemned if one is not baptized! All Scriptures agree to this conclusion. Since we are not condemned for not being baptized, then what does the opposite mean when Mark says,

> *"He that believeth AND is baptized shall be saved?*

It is easy to understand this verse when the child of God realizes there are TWO who recognize that he is justified as being saved. The *"believing"* in Mark 16:16 justifies the person in the eyes of God, as being saved. This is our POSITION in God's eyes, our salvation by belief or faith, only.

Their public baptism is their TESTIMONY, justifying them as being saved in the EYES OF MAN. The lost will not recognize and justify a person as being a child of God, unless he hears the testimony AND sees the works compatible to a Christian. Baptism declares,

> *"For I am not ashamed of the gospel of Christ: for it is the power of God unto salvation...."* (Romans 1:16a).

This identification is justification in man's eyes that I am saved. *"Believeth"* in Mark 16:16 is to the Book of

Romans what baptism is to the Book of James. Romans 4:5 says,

> *"But to him that worketh not, but believeth on him that justifieth the ungodly, his faith is counted for righteousness* (Justification in God's eyes)." (No baptism here!)

Notice James 2:17,18 where man cannot see our faith, unless it is outwardly evidenced.

> *"Even so faith, if it hath not works, is dead,* (in man's eyes) *being alone. Yea, a man may say, Thou hast faith, and I have works: shew me thy faith without thy works, and I will shew thee my faith by my works."* (Justification in man's eyes)."

Therefore, *"he that believeth"* in Mark 16:16 justifies me in GOD'S EYES as being saved AND my baptism justifies me as being saved in MAN'S EYES. *"Believeth"* is my POSITION before God; whereas, baptism is my WALK and TESTIMONY before men.

Luther is as crafty and deceitful as they come as he employs his tactics of using only pieces of a verse; therefore, *disregarding the context* of the verse. This violates all principles of Biblical interpretation, and indoctrinates a person with a *false peace* predicated on Luther's philosophy of baptismal regeneration. This is why it is important to heed God's warning as given in Ephesians 4:14,

> *"That we henceforth be no more children, tossed to and fro, and carried about with every wind of doctrine, by*

> *the sleight* (i.e. trickery) *of men, and cunning craftiness, whereby they lie in wait to deceive;"*

Mark 16:16 contains 17 words. Luther quotes 9 of the 17, and omits the last 8 words. This is one of the devices every cult leader uses to deceive their followers. Luther has earned and well deserves, by his own writings, the title of THE MASTER OF DECEIT.

Luther's faith is in water baptism, a work of the flesh. This is Satan's counterfeit of God's Salvation. It comes down to a very simple decision. Who are you going to believe? Is it the Bible or the writings of a man who has been dead for some 460 years? Faith in Jesus Christ and Him alone is God's promise of eternal life; whereas, Luther's false promise of baptismal regeneration leads only to eternal damnation.

- **Luther's Fourth "Sugar Stick" is I Peter 3:21:**

> **"Baptism doth also now save us." I Peter 3:21.** (*Luther's Small Catechism*, P.175, Par. 634).

The above quotation is exactly as it appears in Luther's Catechism. The problem with Luther's quote is that he only quoted 6 words from Verse 21, which contains a total of 36 words. He, then, gave a verse reference that makes it appear he had quoted the complete verse. Luther just chopped 6 words out of a verse to make it support his perverted theology. Is it any wonder why Luther wants you to study his Catechisms, instead of encouraging you to read the Bible for yourself. His instruction to every Lutheran is stated in his *Large Catechism*, P.4, Par.11.

> **"For this reason alone you should eagerly read, recite, ponder, and practice the CATECHISM."**

Now we are going to quote from the Bible, ALL of I Peter 3:21, as well as I Peter 3:20, which gives us the context about which God is speaking.

> *"...When once the longsuffering of God waited in the days of Noah, while the ark was a preparing, wherein few, that is, eight souls were saved by* (through) *water."* (I Peter 3:20).
>
> *The like figure whereunto even baptism doth also now save us (not the putting away of the filth of the flesh* [i.e., our sins]*, but the answer of a good conscience toward God,) by the resurrection of Jesus Christ:"* (I Peter 3:21).

Several years ago, my wife and I were listening to the car radio, having just tuned in to a religious broadcast. After a few minutes, the minister quoted one sentence from I Peter 3:21, that being *"The like figure whereunto even baptism doth also now save us"*—period! He did not finish the verse, but went on to explain at great length the necessity of baptism for salvation.

Again, I cannot emphasize strongly enough the importance of reading *all* of a verse, including the surrounding context, to receive the correct interpretation and meaning. In II Timothy 2:15 we are instructed to *"Rightly divide the word of truth"*, NOT "Rightly chop up the word of truth" to make each piece fit a person's preconceived ideas!

Since Verse 21 begins with *"The like figure..."*, it is referring to that which is set forth in Verse 20. It should be noticed that in Verse 20, the "*eight souls that were saved by water*" should be translated "saved through water," NOT "by water." The eight were saved from the flood waters by being *in the ark*—a type of Christ. They were not saved *by* the water, for it was the water which *destroyed*!

Therefore, "*the like figure*" is figurative of the Ark of Christ, which provided absolute safety from the flood waters of death. The flood waters testify of death; and, the ark testifies of resurrection. Notice Genesis 8:4,

> *"And the ark rested in the <u>seventh</u> <u>month</u>, on the <u>seventeenth</u> <u>day</u> of the month, upon the mountains of Ararat."*

It is not by chance that the ark, a type of Christ, rested on the mountain on the 7th month and 17th day. Centuries later, God changed the calendar. Noah's calendar was in effect until the emancipation of Israel from Egypt. God then instituted their religious calendar.

The first month of Israel's religious calendar was the same as the 7th month of Noah' s secular calendar, or our April. The Jewish Passover, representing Christ's death, was on the 14th day (Leviticus 23:4,5); therefore, Christ was resurrected three days later on the 17th, the same day that the ark rested on the mountains of Ararat, showing resurrection.

Conclusion: Baptism does not save us; but, publicly identifies us, showing our faith is in the death, and resurrection of our Savior, the Lord Jesus Christ.

Returning to I Peter 3:21, we find the phrase *"baptism doth also now save us"* is explained within the verse, itself. Here we have the "negative" and the "positive." The "negative" tells us what baptism *does not* save us from. Here is the record...

> *"...(not the putting away of the filth of the flesh* [i.e., our sins]..."

Now the "positive" telling us what baptism *does* save us from; that being a GUILTY CONSCIENCE before God. Again, the record...

> *"...but the answer of a good conscience toward God,) by the resurrection of Jesus Christ:"*

How simple the Scriptures are when we are willing to accept God' s Word as our authority. A child of God is saved by faith alone (Ephesians 2:8,9); but, will be void of a good, clear conscience until they are willing to be identified with Christ by their public baptism.

Luther is truly one of Satan's prized possessions! He has well-earned the title he deserves, the "Master of Deceit", by not believing Proverbs 30:5, which tells us,

"Every word of God is pure..."

- **Luther's Fifth "Sugar Stick" is Acts 22:16:**

(Luther's *Small Catechism*, P. 175, Par. 630).

"And now why tarriest thou? arise, and be baptized, and wash away thy sins, calling on the name of the Lord."

Only what is underlined appears in Luther's Catechism. Should a person open their Bible and read this verse, one could only conclude that baptism was essential for salvation. The only problem with this is, that it would contradict all of the multiplicity of Scriptures that promise eternal life by belief, faith, and the blood of Christ, *excluding* baptism.

The person in question is the Apostle Paul. The verse in question is that of Acts 22:16 stating, "*... arise, and be baptized, and wash away thy sins,...*" We have the person and the verse in question; now, we seek to answer the most important question, "Does faith in Christ *alone* save, or is it baptism that saves?" To reach a definite conclusion, let us briefly examine Paul's life in three areas, which will bring us back to the answer to Acts 22:16. The three areas are: Paul's PAST Reputation; Paul's PRESENT Redemption; and Paul's FUTURE Response.

Paul's PAST Reputation.

Let's allow the Scriptures to speak for themselves. In Acts 7, Stephen was being stoned to death for his faith in Jesus Christ. Paul was part of it. Verse 58 states,

1. *"And cast him* (Stephen) *out of the city, and stoned him: and the witnesses laid down their clothes at a young man's feet, whose name was Saul."*

2. In Acts 8:1a, *"And Saul was consenting unto his death...."*

3. In Acts 9:1, *"And Saul, yet breathing out threatenings and slaughter against the disciples of the Lord..."*

4. Galatians 1:13, *"For ye have heard of my conversation in time past in the Jews' religion, how that beyond measure I persecuted the church of God, and wasted it:"*

Here are Paul's words when he was arrested in Jerusalem, concerning his past.

> *"And I persecuted this way* (i.e., Christians) *unto the death, binding and delivering into prisons both men and women."* (Acts 22:4).

Paul's past, in summary, documented him as a *blasphemer;* a *persecutor*; and a *murderer* of Christians.

Paul's PRESENT Redemption:

In Acts, Chapter 9, we have recorded Paul's encounter with Jesus Christ as he was on his way to Damascus. It was at this meeting when Paul got saved. The record is found in Acts 9:3-6.

> *"And as he journeyed, he came near Damascus: and suddenly there shined round about him a light from heaven:"* (V.3)
>
> *"And he fell to the earth, and heard a voice saying unto him, Saul, Saul, why persecutest thou me?"* (V.4).
>
> *"And he said, Who art thou, Lord? And the Lord said, I am Jesus whom thou persecutest: it is hard for thee to kick against the pricks."* (V.5).
>
> *"And he trembling and astonished said, Lord, what wilt thou have me to do? And the Lord said unto him, Arise, and go into the city, and it shall be told thee what thou must do."* (V.6).

It is important to realize that the Greek word for "Lord" is *"Kurios."* The first translation of the Old Testament Scriptures into Greek was known as the Septuagint. Whenever the translators came to translate the Hebrew word "*Jehovah,*" i.e. "*GOD*", into the Greek, they used *"Kurios."* Paul knew Hebrew and Greek well; as "Paul" is his Greek name and "Saul" is his Hebrew name. He was known by both. Therefore, when the Lord asked Saul in Verse 4,

> *"...Why persecutest thou me?"*

He thought it was Jehovah GOD, speaking. In Verse 5, Saul answered,

> *"...Who art thou, Lord?"* (i.e., "Kurios," Greek for "Jehovah" of the Old Testament).

In other words, "Are you GOD?"

> *"...And the Lord said, I am Jesus whom thou persecutest:"*

Paul immediately recognized that this was Jesus, the Messiah, the Savior, being God manifested in the flesh. In Verse 6 we have Saul's salvation recorded, as he acknowledges Jesus as Jehovah GOD.

> *"And he* (Paul) *trembling and astonished said, Lord,* (Greek, "Kurios", i.e. GOD) *what wilt thou have me to do?*

Paul had now *changed his mind* about Jesus Christ, whom he had previously thought to be a false teacher. He was now SAVED, as he later wrote in Romans 5:1.

> *"Therefore being justified by faith, we have peace with God through our Lord Jesus Christ:"* (No baptism here.)

A short time later, at Damascus, when Ananias met with Paul, he addressed him as *"BROTHER SAUL!"* He was now recognized as a spiritual Christian brother in Christ. (Acts 9:17). Remember, Paul is *now saved*; but, he has not yet been baptized.

Luther disagrees with God's Word, as he states in his Catechism the following:

> **Moreover, it is solemnly and strictly commanded that we must be baptized or we shall not be saved."** (*Large Catechism*, P.81, Par. 6).

Here, again, Luther is found to be a liar and a false teacher, as Saul was already saved prior to his baptism. Always keep in remembrance the *three proofs* of Saul's salvation *prior* to his baptism. May I recapitulate for emphasis.

1. In Acts 9:6 – Saul called Jesus "Lord," proof that he had repented (i.e., Greek, *"metanoeo,"*); or changed his mind concerning Jesus being a false teacher, and He was now his Savior.

2. Also in Acts 9:6 – We find Saul, the persecutor and murderer of those who followed Christ; NOW, wanted to serve the true and living God, Jesus the Messiah. He proved this by making his will known in the statement, *"...What wilt thou have me to do."*

3. Acts 9:17 –Ananias, recognizing that Saul was a *"chosen vessel"* of the Lord in Verse 15, as Jesus had told him. Then in Verse 17, Ananias, upon meeting Saul, addressed him as a brother in Christ by stating, *"BROTHER SAUL."*

❖ Paul's FUTURE Response.

From the time of Paul being saved in Acts, Chapter 9, until we reach Acts, Chapter 22, several years have passed. In the meantime he had made three missionary journeys, which began in Acts 13:2, and culminated in Acts 21:17 with his arrival back in Jerusalem.

Now let us return to our Verse in question, found in Acts 22:16, where Paul is testifying about what Ananias said to him AFTER he was saved.

> *"And now why tarriest thou? arise, and be baptized, and wash away thy sins, calling on the name of the Lord."*

How important it is to examine the context and circumstances of a particular verse, which will always reveal the truth of a subject to the person who will be honest with the Scriptures and themselves. The subject matter in question, of which Acts 22:16 is a part, begins back in Acts 21:15 where Paul goes to Jerusalem. It is here, in the Temple, that the people apprehend Paul.

> *"And all the city was moved, and the people ran together: and they took Paul, and drew him out of the*

> *temple: and forthwith the doors were shut."* (Acts 21:30).

Paul was not in the inner sanctuary (Greek, *"ho naos"*); but, only in the outer court (Greek, "*to hieron*"). The "*Jews from Asia*" had stirred up the people and they were beating Paul when he was saved by the chief captain and soldiers (Acts 21:32). As they were leading him to the barracks, the Roman soldiers' "castle," (Acts 21:37), Paul asked the chief captain for permission to speak to the people. (Acts 21:39,40).

Paul's testimony is recorded in Acts 22:1-21. The content of his testimony was relating what he had experienced earlier, as recorded in Acts, Chapter 9.

Again, it is to be emphasized that Paul's salvation is evidenced by his acknowledgement of Christ as his Lord, or Savior (Acts 22:7,8,10). He also testifies to the fact that Ananias addressed him as a spiritual brother, since both were Christians.

> (Ananias)*"Came unto me, and stood, and said unto me, BROTHER Saul...."* (Acts 22:13).

As noted, only the saved are spiritual brothers and sisters in Christ, and such was Paul. Since Paul was already saved, what did Ananias mean by telling Paul to be,

> *"...baptized and wash away thy sins, calling on the name of the Lord."* (Acts 22:16).

One must remember that there is a JUDICIAL or POSITIONAL justification of sin, and a PRACTICAL justification of sin. When Paul was saved, he received remission for all his sins, JUDICIALLY; i.e., Christ's death on the cross bore the ETERNAL payment for Paul's sins; past, present, and future.

> *"Being justified* (declared absolutely righteous) *freely by his grace through the redemption that is in Christ Jesus: Whom God hath set forth to be a propitiation* (payment) *through faith in his blood* (not baptism*), to declare his righteousness for the remission of sins that are past, through the forbearance of God;"* (Romans 3:24,25).

Ananias was instructing Saul as to how God wanted him to deal with his past sins: PRACTICALLY and PUBLICLY. Almost every Jew and Gentile knew of Paul's commitment and reputation concerning his persecution of Christians.

> *"And Saul, yet breathing out threatenings and slaughter against the disciples of the Lord..."* (Acts 9:1).

> *"And I said, Lord, they know that I imprisoned and beat in every synagogue them that believed on thee:* (V.19).

> *And when the blood of thy martyr Stephen was shed, I also was standing by, and consenting unto his death, and kept the raiment of them that slew him."* (Acts 22:19,20).

Now that Paul is a Christian, his PUBLIC profession of faith in Christ is of utmost importance, just as it is for every Christian. His baptism would be a PUBLIC TESTIMONY of his faith in the death, burial, and resurrection of Jesus Christ. By his baptism, he was now publicly identifying himself with those Christians who he once persecuted.

In baptism, being immersed shows "death," and being raised out of the water shows "resurrection." When Paul was baptized, it was his PUBLIC testimony that he was not the same person he was before he met Christ on the road to Damascus. He later wrote:

> *"Therefore we are buried with him by baptism into death: that like as Christ was raised up from the dead by the glory of the Father, even so we also should walk in newness of life."* (Romans 6:4).

The sins Paul was going to "wash away" were his acts of persecution against Christians prior to being saved. JUDICIALLY, Paul's sins were judged on Calvary; now, they would be "washed away" PUBLICLY in the eyes of the Christians who knew of his conversion (made public by his baptism).

You can rest assured, Paul gave his testimony at his baptism, by calling on the name of the Lord in thanksgiving for saving a sinner such as he! One example can be found in I Timothy 1:12-15,

> *"And I thank Christ Jesus our Lord, who hath enabled me, for that he counted me faithful, putting me into the ministry;* (V.12).

> *"Who was before a blasphemer, and a persecutor, and injurious: but I obtained mercy, because I did it ignorantly in unbelief.* (V.13).
>
> *And the grace of our Lord was exceeding abundant with faith and love which is in Christ Jesus.* (V.14).
>
> *This is a faithful saying, and worthy of all acceptation, that Christ Jesus came into the world to save sinners; of whom I am chief."* (V.15).

The sins of Paul's persecution against Christians WOULD NEVER BE REPEATED AGAIN! His PUBLIC profession, from that time on "WASHED AWAY" any doubt of those sins ever being repeated. God had taken a persecutor and made a preacher; a murderer and made a missionary, and turned a blasphemer into a blessing. God also used Paul to pen 14 of the 27 Epistles of the New Testament.

Yes, JUDICIALLY, Paul's sins were accounted "paid in full" at the cross. PUBLICLY, they were "washed away," as there remained no doubt in people's minds as to where he stood; remaining faithful to his Lord until his death.

I have taken a little more time with Luther's quote of Acts 22:16, *"... arise, and be baptized, and wash away thy sins,"* to show the importance of reading the whole context surrounding a verse. Luther was a MASTER at quoting parts of a verse, and omitting the context, in an attempt to make it support his false teaching of baptismal regeneration.

Acts 22:16 is a classic example of one of Luther's deceptions. For some 460 years, since Luther's death in 1546, his puppet preachers have preached his philosophy, leading untold millions into eternal damnation thinking they are saved by being baptized. I have attended several Lutheran funerals and I hear the same thing, without exception. "REMEMBER THEIR BAPTISM."

Luther labels those who disagree with him as "foolish" and "know-it-alls" in his *Large Catechism*, Page 84. God's answer to Luther, and every other false teacher is this,

> *"Let the lying lips be put to silence; which speak grievous things proudly and contemptuously against the righteous."* (Psalms 31:18).

Luther's "crown jewel" for his pseudo-doctrine of baptismal regeneration turns out to be nothing more than a rhinestone; a piece of cheap glass!"

- **Luther's Sixth "Sugar Stick" is Galatians 3:26,27:**

> **"For ye are all the children of God by *faith* in Christ Jesus. For as many of you as have *been baptized* into Christ have *put on Christ. Gal. 3:26,27"*** (*Luther's Small Catechism*, P.175, Par.631).

This is another one of the "Sugar Stick" verses also used by the Roman Catholic organization which Luther followed. He never broke away from their teaching, as he continued to teach water baptism for salvation, as written in his Catechisms. Here are Luther's own words in his *Small Catechism*, P. 174, last paragraph.

"II. THE BLESSINGS OF BAPTISM

What does baptism give or profit? It works forgiveness of sins, delivers from death and the devil, and gives eternal salvation to all who believe this."

As we examine Luther's claims, we find that the words and promises of God DO NOT declare or promise any such claims as stated in the above paragraph. All one has to do is to read Galatians, Chapter 3, completely; as the entire chapter is presenting, "salvation by FAITH alone," as contrasted to the "works of the law;" or, any good works done out of the flesh.

Baptism is a WORK, defined as such, because Luther is trusting in that human effort for righteousness in order to be saved. In examining the surrounding verses, it becomes very evident that Galatians 3:27 is speaking of SPIRITUAL baptism and not of water baptism. When we place our FAITH in Jesus Christ, and Him alone for our salvation, we are instantaneously placed INTO i.e., baptized into the *Spiritual Body of Christ.*

Paul is writing under the direction of the Holy Spirit concerning this same Spiritual baptism, that is also recorded in I Corinthians.

> *"For by one Spirit are we all baptized into one body, whether we be Jews or Gentiles, whether we be bond or free; and have been all made to drink into one Spirit."* (I Corinthians 12:13).

This verse does NOT say, "for by the WATER are we all baptized into one body"; but, "*for by ONE SPIRIT*." Notice that Paul uses the same language in Galatians in reference to SPIRITUAL baptism as he does in I Corinthians.

> *"For as many of you as have been baptized* (i.e., Spiritually) *into Christ have put on Christ. There is neither Jew nor Greek, there is neither bond nor free, there is neither male nor female: for ye are all one in Christ Jesus."* (Galatians 3:27).

Notice the underlined words, "*have put on Christ.*" The question some may ask is, "How have I put on Christ, now that I am saved by FAITH in Jesus Christ?" God's Word gives the answer. There are two additional promises that God fulfills, in addition to placing the believer into the Spiritual Body of Christ. The one is *internal* and the other is *external.* All three take place simultaneously with salvation by FAITH in Christ Jesus.

❖ *The External by Relationship: "Children of God"*

> *"For ye are all the children of God by faith in Christ Jesus."* (Galatians 3:26).

This agrees perfectly with all other Scriptures concerning salvation. We have "*put on Christ*" by being one of His children. We are spiritually related by accepting Christ as our Savior. The Apostle John agrees, as "*All Scripture is given by inspiration of God..*" (II Timothy 3:16). God cannot contradict Himself.

> *"But as many as received him, to them gave he power to become the sons of God, even to them that believe on his name:"* (John 1:12).

Notice carefully that Galatians 3:26 would contradict Galatians 3:27, if the baptism is that of water, instead of spiritual baptism. Remember, God does not contradict Himself; BUT, we cannot say the same thing about Martin Luther, who contradicts himself prolifically!

- ***Internal by Ownership: The Indwelling of the Holy Spirit.***

> *"In whom ye also trusted, after that ye heard the word of truth, the gospel of your salvation: in whom also after that ye believed, ye were sealed with that holy Spirit of promise,"* (Ephesians 1:13).

Upon believing in Christ as one's Savior, that person is SEALED with the Holy Spirit of God, who lives within each and every saved Child of God. This is the new nature that dwells within. This is "ownership" as also stated in Ephesians by the word "SEALED."

> *"And grieve not the holy Spirit of God, whereby ye are sealed unto the day of redemption."*(Ephesians 4:30).

Now, let us analyze and compare a few of the Scriptures that expose Luther as the "Master of Deceit.," who desires to sift you into believing that your baptism will take you to Heaven. Instead, it is nothing more than a TRAP DOOR TO HELL!

❖ *God's Word Exposes Luther's Deceit.*

1. **Galatians 3:26.** *"For ye are all the children of God by faith in Christ Jesus."* (Not baptism).

2. **Galatians 3:24.** *"Wherefore the law was our school-master to bring us unto Christ, that we might be justified by faith."* (Not baptism.)

3. **Galatians 3:6**. *"Even as Abraham believed God, and it was accounted to him for righteousness."* (No baptism here.)

4. **Galatians 1:3,4a**. *"Grace be to you and peace from God the Father, and from our Lord Jesus Christ, Who gave himself for our sins,..."* (No baptism here.)

5. **Galatians 2:16**. *"Knowing that a man is not justified by the works of the law, but by the faith of* (in) *Jesus Christ, even we have believed in Jesus Christ, that we might be justified by the faith of* (in) *Christ, and not by the works of the law: for by the works of the law shall no flesh be justified."*

Here, faith and belief in Christ produces *justification,* NOT BAPTISM. (No baptism here.)

6. **Galatians 3:9**. *"So then they which be of faith are blessed with faithful Abraham."* (No baptism here.)

7. **Galatians 3:11**. *"But that no man is justified by the law in the sight of God, it is evident: for, The just shall live by faith."* (No baptism here.)

I have heard many layman and Christian pastors quote Luther as saying "The just shall live by faith." They are, therefore, misled into believing that Luther was a Christian and thinking that he believed the same as they do. Nothing could be further from the truth! It is evident they have never read Luther's Catechisms; but, have passed on the rumors they have heard.

What Luther *means* when he states that "The just shall live by faith," is FAITH IN WATER BAPTISM FOR SALVATION! Should one doubt this, let me allow Luther to speak again for himself in his *Large Catechism*.

> **"In Baptism, therefore, every Christian has enough to study and practice all his life. He always has enough to do to believe firmly what Baptism promises and brings—Victory over death and the devil, forgiveness of sin, God's grace, the entire Christ, and the Holy Spirit with his gifts."** (*Large Catechism*, P, 86, Par. 41).

God will now speak for *Himself* in Ephesians 1:7.

"In whom we have redemption through his (Christ's) *blood, the forgiveness of sins, according to the riches of his grace;"*

Luther is in competition with God over who is going to have the authority over your life. We have just quoted Luther in his *Large Catechism*; saying that Baptism provides forgiveness of sin; BUT, God says that we have forgiveness of sins through the BLOOD of Christ, NOT the water. Who are you going to believe, Luther, a dead man for 460 years; or Jesus Christ, the true and living Savior?

(Ephesians 2:8,9). *"For by grace are ye saved through faith; and that not of yourselves: it is the gift of God: Not of works, lest any man should boast."*

Luther denies Ephesians 2:8,9 and contradicts the Word of God by stating you do not have to have faith to be saved; just be baptized. Again, we allow Luther to speak for himself.

"Further, we are not primarily concerned whether the baptized person believes or not, for in the latter case, Baptism does NOT become invalid." (*Large Catechism*, P. 87, Par. 52).

"Baptism is valid, even though FAITH be lacking." (Par. 53).

> **"Even though a Jew should today come deceitfully and with an evil purpose, and we baptized him in all good faith, we should have to admit that his BAPTISM WAS VALID."** (Par. 53).

God never contradicts himself; BUT, false teachers continually attempt to contradict God. The Lord would have us to know that:

> *"All scripture is given by inspiration of God, and is profitable for doctrine, for reproof, for correction, for instruction in righteousness:"* (II Timothy 3:16).

Paul would not have told the Ephesians they were saved "*by grace through faith,*" and then told the Galatians they were saved by water baptism.

Conclusion: All Scriptures agree that Galatians 3:27 is spiritual baptism and NOT water baptism.

- **Luther's Seventh "Sugar Stick" is Romans 6:3:**

> **"IT (BAPTISM) DELIVERS FROM DEATH AND THE DEVIL."**

> ***"Know ye not, that so many of us as were baptized into Jesus Christ were baptized into his death?* Rom. 6:3."** (*Luther's Small Catechism,* P.175, Par. 632).

Will someone show me *anything* in this verse that Luther says, "Delivers me from death and the devil?" It does not exist. Here again, Luther violates all principles of Biblical Studies by: (1). Quoting one verse out of context, (2). Failing to compare it with other Scriptures, (3). And then telling you what the verse means, which CONTRADICTS what the verse plainly says!

Where do you find that "baptism delivers from death" in this verse? Where do you find "baptism delivers from the devil" in this verse? And where do you find the word "deliver" in this verse? And where do you find the word "devil" in this verse? Romans 6:3, which Luther quotes in his Catechism to lead you to believe that baptism saves you, contains <u>none</u> of the above.

- ***An Examination of God's Word Reveals Luther's Claim That Baptism Gives Salvation Is Totally False.***

For Luther's false claims to be true, ALL Scriptures that deal with salvation would have to include baptism. Let us examine a few of the verses in just the first five chapters of Romans, itself, and see if they agree with Luther's idea of salvation by baptism.

1. **Romans 1:16**. *"For I am not ashamed of the gospel of Christ* (i.e., death and resurrection)*: for it is the power of God unto salvation to every one that <u>believeth</u>; ..."* (No baptism here.)

2. **Romans 1:17**. *"The just shall live by <u>faith</u>."* (Not baptism.)

3. **Romans 3:22.** *"Even the righteousness of God which is by faith of Jesus Christ unto all and upon all them that believe: for there is no difference:"* (No baptism here.)

4. **Romans 3:24.** *"Being justified* (i.e., declared righteous) *freely by his grace through the redemption that is in Christ Jesus:"* (No baptism here.)

5. **Romans 3:25.** *"Whom God hath set forth to be a propitiation* (i.e., payment) *through faith in his* (Christ's) *blood, to declare his righteousness for the remission of sins that are past, through the forbearance of God;"* (No baptism here.)

6. **Romans 3:26**. *"To declare, I say, at this time his righteousness: that he might be just, and the justifier of him which believeth in Jesus."* (No baptism here.)

7. **Romans 3:28**. *"Therefore we conclude that a man is justified by faith without the deeds of the law."* (No baptism here.)

8. **Romans 3:30**. *"Seeing it is one God, which shall justify the circumcision* (the Jews) *by faith, and uncircumcision* (the Gentiles) through *faith*." (No baptism here.)

9. **Romans 4:3**. *"For what saith the scripture? Abraham believed God, and it was counted unto him for righteousness."* (No baptism here.)

10. **Romans 4:5**. *"But to him that worketh not, but believeth on him that justifieth the ungodly, his faith is counted for righteousness."* (No baptism here.)

11. **Romans 4:13**. *"For the promise, that he should be the heir of the world, was not to Abraham, or to his seed, through the law, but through the righteousness of faith."* (No baptism here.)

12. **Romans 5:1**. *"Therefore being justified by faith, we have peace with God through our Lord Jesus Christ:"* (No baptism here.)

13. **Romans 5:9.** *"Much more then, being now justified by his blood, we shall be saved from wrath through him (Christ)."* (No baptism here.)

14. **Romans 5:10**. *"...we were reconciled to God by the death of his Son, much more, being reconciled, we shall be saved by his life."* (No baptism here.)

15. **Romans 5:11**. *"...but we also joy in God through our Lord Jesus Christ, by whom we have now received the atonement* (i.e., reconciliation)."(No baptism here.)

In Romans 5:15-18, we find these four verses speak of salvation as a FREE GIFT, as also does Romans 6:23. Baptism is a work of the flesh, a fact which Luther does not want you to believe. The gift of eternal life is what Christ purchased on the cross. He offers this gift to "whosoever will" receive it by FAITH, not by the work of the flesh with the water.

16. **Romans 5:21.***"That as sin hath reigned unto death, even so might grace reign through righteousness unto eternal life by Jesus Christ our Lord."* (No baptism here.)

The preceding verses are just the tip of the iceberg of the hundreds that could be given. Luther, if tried in God's court of justice, would be found guilty by God's Word and receive the sentence of all unbelievers and deceitful workers.

> *"Then shall he say also unto them on the left hand, Depart from me, ye cursed, into everlasting fire, prepared for the devil and his angels:"* (Matthew 25:41).

Should one choose to believe Luther's writings over the infallible Word of God, then there is nothing more the Lord can do; but, honor your decision and conclude:

> *"But if any man be ignorant, let him be ignorant."* (I Corinthians 14:38).

In examining the first five chapters of Romans, we have found no mention of baptism, whatsoever. These chapters are dealing with our salvation, as shown by the sixteen verses you have just read. Now we come to Romans, Chapter Six, where the whole chapter is dealing with the Christian's life AFTER they are saved. Paul, in Romans 6:1,2, reveals God's will concerning our behavior as a Christian.

> *"What shall we say then? Shall we continue in sin, that grace may abound?"*(V.1).

> *"God forbid. How shall we, that are dead to sin, live any longer therein?"*(V.2).

Paul then reminds the Christian of what their public baptism was a testimony of. In other words, by being put under the water, which represents death; and being raised out of the water, which represents resurrection; it is the Christian's public testimony. It shows, symbolically, that their faith is in the death and resurrection of Jesus Christ for their salvation.

Baptism also is a testimony that one is not the same person as they were. "Once I was lost; but, now I am saved," as described in II Corinthians 5:17.

> *"Therefore if any man be in Christ, he is a new creature* (Greek, "creation"): *old things are passed away; behold, all things are become new."*

This is my POSITION in Christ. This is how Christ looks upon the Christian at the moment they are saved. Now that I am a Christian, the Lord wants me to follow him and WALK like a Christian. This is what Paul describes in Romans 6:3,4.

> *"Know ye not, that so many of us as were baptized into Jesus Christ were baptized into his death?"* (V.3)

> *"Therefore we are buried with him by baptism into death: that like as Christ was raised up from the dead by the glory of the Father, even so we also should walk in newness of life."* (V.4)

I hope one can begin to see how deceptive this man, Martin Luther, really is. He totally disregards the first five chapters of Romans that teach salvation is through Jesus Christ and *Him alone*. He totally disregards the whole context of Romans 6 dealing with the Christian's WALK after they are saved. He then extracts Romans 6:3, completely out of context, in an attempt to deceive you into thinking that baptism saves you.

In conclusion: We have God's Word as a warning concerning Luther and all false teachers who PERVERT the Gospel. The Lord addresses these false teachers in Galatians 1:6,7.

> *"I marvel that ye are so soon removed from him* (Christ) *that called you into the grace of Christ unto another gospel:* (V.6)
>
> *Which is not another; but there be some that trouble you, and would pervert the gospel of Christ."* (V.7).

Notice the word "another" which occurs twice in Galatians 1:6,7. When you look these two words up in the Greek, it gives us a little better understanding. They are translated from two different Greek words. In Verse 6, "*another*" is the Greek word "*heteros,"* i.e., a different Gospel. Then, in Verse 7, "*which is not another*," (Greek, "*allos*") Gospel *like* the one Paul preached. In other words, this was a different Gospel, a false Gospel.

Notice the word "*pervert*" in Verse 7. It is from the Greek word "*metastrepho.*" "*Meta*" signifies a change, and "*strepho*", to turn. In other words, these false teachers would change the truth and turn it into a lie. Martin Luther is a perfect example of someone who does this.

- ❖ THE TRUTH, in God's Word concerning salvation.

  "In whom we have redemption through his blood, the forgiveness of sins, according to the riches of his grace;" (Ephesians 1:7).

- ❖ THE LIE, in Luther's Catechism concerning Salvation.

  "...We accept the forgiveness, life, and salvation offered in Baptism and make these blessings our own." (Small Catechism, P. 177, Par. 257).

As one can see, Luther has taken the truth, "salvation by the blood," as stated in God's Word; and turned it into the lie of "salvation by water baptism," as he states in his Catechism.

- ❖ GOD'S WARNING, concerning the false teachers.

  "Now I beseech you, brethren, mark them which cause divisions and offences contrary to the doctrine which ye have learned; and avoid them.(V.17).

  For they that are such serve not our Lord Jesus Christ, but their own belly; and by good words and fair speeches deceive the hearts of the simple." (Romans 16:17,18).

- ALWAYS REMEMBER the "middle verse of the Bible."

"It is better to trust in the LORD than to put confidence in man." (Psalm 118:8).

How can Luther fool so many people? When you talk to Lutherans, you will find that many believe that Christ died and was resurrected as payment for their sins, AND that they have been baptized. Upon being told this, the Christian assumes they are saved just as we are, and then the conversation proceeds no further!

Luther, in his Catechism, states the following:

"I believe that Jesus Christ, true God, begotten of the Father from eternity, and also true man, born of the Virgin Mary, is my Lord, who has redeemed me, a lost and condemned creature, purchased and won me from all sins, from death, and from the power of the devil; not with gold or silver, but with His holy, precious blood and with His innocent suffering and death, that I may be His own, and live under Him in His kingdom, and serve Him in everlasting righteousness, innocence, and blessedness, even as He is risen from the dead, lives and reigns to all eternity." (*Small Catechism*, P.100).

Now, if Luther had stopped right here, he would have believed Christ's last words on the cross and have been saved. Christ's last words on the cross were,

> *"When Jesus therefore had received the vinegar, he said, It is FINISHED: and he bowed his head, and gave up the ghost."* (John 19:30).

But, sad to say, Luther *did not* stop here. He did not believe that trusting Christ, and Him ALONE, was sufficient for obtaining salvation. Luther believed that Christ and His sufferings and death on the cross *only earned eternal salvation* and its blessings for us. Although Christ had purchased our salvation and forgiveness of sins by his shed BLOOD on Calvary, it does not go into effect UNTIL we are baptized. Let Luther verify his claims for himself.

> **"But has not Christ earned all these blessings for us?"**
>
> **"By His suffering and death Christ has indeed EARNED these blessings for us; BAPTISM, however, is a means by which the Holy Spirit makes these blessings our own, (Baptism is a means of grace)."** (*Small Catechism,* P. 175, Par. 254).

Luther was never a saved man. He did not believe Christ when He said, *"It is finished."* He believed ABOUT Christ; BUT, he did not believe IN Christ and Him alone for his salvation. The reason Luther did not trust Christ and Him ALONE, is recorded in his Catechism.

> **"Our know-it-alls, the new spirits** (i.e., those who disagree with Luther)**, assert that faith alone saves and that works and external things contribute nothing to this end...faith must have something to believe—something to which it may cling and upon which it may stand. Thus faith clings to the WATER and believes it to be Baptism, in which there is sheer SALVATION and life..."** (*Large Catechism*, P. 84, Par. 28,29).

One must recognize that no one for four-thousand years, from Adam and Eve to John the Baptist, were ever baptized! Of the two criminals that were crucified with Christ, both mocked Him for the first three hours while on the cross. (Matthew 27:44,45). After three hours, one of the criminals repented (i.e., changed his mind), and realized that this Jesus beside him was truly the Savior of the world.

> *"And he said unto Jesus, Lord, remember me when thou comest into thy kingdom." (Luke 23:42).*

You cannot possess a kingdom, unless you are a king. He knew Christ was the King of Kings and Lord of Lords. He was saved the moment he believed, as Christ immediately assured him of that. Here is the record.

> *"And Jesus said unto him, Verily I say unto thee, To day shalt thou be with me in paradise."* (Luke 23:43).

He spent the next three hours on the cross beside his Savior, the Lord Jesus. (Luke 23:44) He possessed eternal life for his faith in Christ; BUT, he was NEVER baptized!

His testimony lives on today!

Chapter Eight

Unmasking One of Satan's Choice Ambassadors

- ***Did you know?***

"**Few people are more misunderstood in America than Martin Luther**. For most Americans Luther is seen as a kind of German counterpart to America's founding fathers, fighting for free speech and religious tolerance. Nothing could be further from the truth.

Luther's courageous and vital role in successfully toppling the Catholic Church from its dominant position in Europe did **not** lead to a world view that endorsed civil liberties. Luther's replacement for the Catholic church in Germany was a religious system dominated by the power of the German kings and princes, the beginning of a process of political fragmentation in Germany that would lead to the Thirty Years War, and one of the greatest disasters in modern European history where one third of all the German people would perish under appalling circumstances.

The legal structure of the Lutheran church in Germany, which he created, would be a major factor in Nazi Germany. The Lutheran pastors were employees of the Prussian state. In other words they got their paychecks from Hitler.

Luther was a man consumed by various hatreds. His hatred of the Catholic Church was accompanied by an equally **virulent hatred of both democracy and the Jews**. During the peasants revolt Luther called for the most ferocious measures possible by the German nobles to wipe out the power of the peasants.

Luther was totally opposed to the idea of religious freedom. Had a modem American evangelist like Billy Graham come to Saxony, he would not have met a happy fate. Luther hated the Baptists and urged that they be executed. Luther also strongly supported the use of the death penalty for many other Christian "heresies."

In his vitriolic book, *The Jews and Their Lies,* Luther called for the expulsion of the Jews from Germany, and actually succeeded in convincing his patron, the Elector of Saxony, to expel all Jews from his territory. It is almost certain that the Nazis got the idea for Kristall Nacht from Luther since **he very specifically called for the burning down of all synagogues in Germany.** The Nazis carried out Luther's wishes on his birthday in 1938.

Horrible and criminal as Luther's ideas were, it is very important to see that they were hardly isolated points of view. The British and the French monarchies had already adopted such policies during the High Middle Ages. In 1492 the Spanish monarchy carried out the appalling expulsion of over 300,000 Jews as well as committing a long series of war crimes against its Islamic subjects.

In fairness, Luther did not call for the total extermination of the Jews. However, there is no doubt he paved the way for this crime. Hitler repeatedly compared himself to Luther, and his works were reprinted and distributed all over Germany by the Nazis." (www.worldfuturefund.org)

That Luther hated the Jews.

The following are some excerpts from the "*Medieval Sourcebook: Martin Luther (1483-1546) The Jews and their Lies, Excerpts (1543).*"

1. "Therefore the blind Jews are truly stupid fools...

2. Now just behold these miserable, blind, and senseless people.

3. Therefore be on your guard against the Jews, knowing that wherever they have their synagogues, nothing is found but a den of devils in which sheer self-glory, conceit, lies, blasphemy, and defaming of God and men are practiced most maliciously and veheming his eyes on them.

4. Did I not tell you earlier that a Jew is such a noble, precious jewel that God and all the angels dance when he farts?

5. No, one should toss out these lazy rogues by the seat of their pants.

6. ...but then eject them forever from this country. For, as we have heard, God's anger with them is so intense that gentle mercy will only tend to make them worse and worse, while sharp mercy will reform them but little. Therefore, in any case, away with them!

7. I brief, dear princes and lords, those of you who have Jews under your rule-- if my counsel does not please you, find better advice, so that you and we all can be

rid of the unbearable, devilish burden of the Jews, lest we become guilty sharers before God in the lies, blasphemy, the defamation, and the curses which the mad Jews indulge in so freely and wantonly against the person of our Lord Jesus Christ, this dear mother, all Christians, all authority, and ourselves. Do not grant them protection, safe-conduct, or communion with us.... .With this faithful counsel and warning I wish to cleanse and exonerate my conscience.

8. Let the government deal with them in this respect, as I have suggested. But whether the government acts or not, let everyone at least be guided by his own conscience and form for himself a definition or image of a Jew.

9. However, we must avoid confirming them in their wanton lying, slandering, cursing, and defaming. Nor dare we make ourselves partners in their devilish ranting and raving by shielding and protecting them, by giving them food, drink, and shelter, or by other neighborly deeds.

10. ...I shall give you my sincere advice:

First, to set fire to their synagogues or schools and to bury and cover with dirt whatever will not burn, so that no man will ever again see a stone or cinder of them...

Second, I advise that their houses also be razed and destroyed. For they pursue in them the same aims as in their synagogues. Instead they might be lodged under a roof or in a barn, like the gypsies. This will bring home to them that they are not masters in our country...

Third, I advise that all their prayer books and Talmudic writings, in which such idolatry, lies, cursing and blasphemy are taught, be taken from them.

Fourth, I advise that their rabbis be forbidden to teach...

Fifth, I advise that safe-conduct on the highways be abolished completely for the Jews. For they have no business in the countryside, since they are not lords, officials, tradesmen, or the like. Let them stay at home.

Sixth, I advise that usury be prohibited to them, and that all cash and treasure of silver and gold be taken from them and put aside for safekeeping. The reason for such a measure is that, as said above, they have no other means of earning a livelihood than usury, and by it they have stolen and robbed from us all they possess. Such money should now be used in no other way than the following: Whenever a Jew is sincerely converted, he should be handed one hundred, two hundred, or three hundred florins, as personal circumstances may suggest. With this he could set himself up in some occupation for the support of his poor wife and children, and the maintenance of the old or feeble. For such evil gains are cursed if they are not put to use with God's blessing in a good and worthy cause.

Seventh, I commend putting a flail, an ax, a hoe, a spade, a distaff, or a spindle into the hands of young, strong Jews and Jewesses and letting them earn their bread in the sweat of their brow, as was imposed on the children of Adam

(Gen 3:19}. For it is not fitting that they should let us accursed Goyim toil in the sweat of our faces while they, the holy people, idle away their time behind the stove, feasting and farting, and on top of all, boasting blasphemously of their lordship over the Christians by means of our sweat. No, one should toss out these lazy rogues by the seat of their pants.

11. But what will happen even if we do burn down the Jews' synagogues and forbid them publicly to praise God, to pray, to teach, to utter God's name? They will still keep doing it in secret...

12. Accordingly, it must and dare not be considered a trifling matter but a most serious one to seek counsel against this and to save our souls from the Jews, that is, from the devil and from eternal death. My advice, as I said earlier, is: First, that their synagogues be burned down, and that all who are able toss in sulphur and pitch; it would be good if someone could also throw in some hellfire. That would demonstrate to God our serious resolve and be evidence to all the world that it was in ignorance that we tolerated such houses, in which the Jews have reviled God, our dear Creator and Father, and his Son most shamefully up till now but that we have now given them their due reward.

13. I wish and I ask that our rulers who have Jewish subjects exercise a sharp mercy toward these wretched people, as suggested above, to see whether this might not help (though it is doubtful). They must act like a good physician who, when gangrene has set in, proceeds without mercy to cut, saw, and burn flesh, veins, bone, and marrow. Such a procedure must also be followed in this instance. Burn down their synagogues, forbid all that I enumerated

earlier, force them to work, and deal harshly with them, as Moses did in the wilderness, slaying three thousand lest the whole people perish. They surely do not know what they are doing; moreover, as people possesed, they do not wish to know it, hear it, or learn it. There it would be wrong to be merciful and confirm them in their conduct. If this does not help we must drive them out like mad dogs, so that we do not become partakers of their abominable blasphemy and all their other vices and thus merit God's wrath and be damned with them. I have done my duty. Now let everyone see to his. I am exonerated."

These, my dear friend, are the words of Martin Luther, Master of Deceit! It amazes me how anyone who believes the Bible would even consider being identified with Martin Luther, his philosophy, and his hatred for God's chosen people, the Jews. This man has been dead for over 460 years and Satan loves Luther for hating the Jews, just as he does.

- ***Luther's Attitude Toward Children.***

Luther's philosophy was, "It is my way or the highway!" If you didn't obey Luther, you were to be punished. I would like to draw your attention to Luther's *Large Catechism*, on Pages 6 and 7. Luther states that the most necessary parts of Christian instruction are as he lists them, which your children better memorize or be punished!

- **"THE TEN COMMANDMENTS OF GOD."**

Luther then lists ten commandments. Has your pastor taught you that Luther lied, when he said "the Ten

Commandments OF GOD." If all the Ten Commandments given by Luther were of God; then why don't we find the Second Commandment in Luther's list?

Open your Bible to Exodus 20:3-17, where God's Ten Commandments are given and you will discover in Verses 4 and 5, the Second Commandment of God, which Luther omitted in his Catechisms. Then, to cover his deceit, he takes the Tenth Commandment and makes two commandments out of it. He then lies to you, saying that these are God's Ten Commandments. How deceptive and Satanic!

- **"THE CHIEF ARTICLES OF OUR FAITH"**

It contains 107 words. I have quoted it below; but, you may read it for yourself on Page 7 of the *Large Catechism.*

> **"1. I believe in God the Father Almighty, Maker of heaven and earth.**
>
> **2. And in Jesus Christ, His only Son, our Lord; who was conceived by the Holy Ghost, born of the Virgin Mary; suffered under Pontius Pilate, was crucified, dead and buried; He descended into hell; the third day He rose again from the dead; He ascended into heaven, and sitteth on the right hand of God the Father Almighty; from thence He shall come to judge the quick and the dead.**

3. I believe in the Holy Ghost, the holy Christian Church, the communion of saints, the forgiveness of sins, the resurrection of the body, and the life everlasting. Amen."

- **THE PRAYER, OR "OUR FATHER," WHICH CHRIST TAUGHT.**

Essentially, this is the Lord's Prayer as in Matthew 6:9-15. This is composed of approximately 71 words.

"...Our Father who art in heaven,

1. **Hallowed be thy name.**
2. **Thy kingdom come.**
3. **Thy will be done on earth, as *it is* in heaven.**
4. **Give us this day our daily bread.**

5. **And forgive us our trespasses, as we forgive those who trespass against us.**

6. **And lead us not into temptation,**
7. **But deliver us from evil: [For Thine is the kingdom, and the power, and the glory, forever and ever.] Amen."**

Contrary to the opinion of a few ignorant people, Martin Luther was not a kind, nice, loving man; but, rather mean and cruel when it involved religion. After listing the above three parts as Luther gives in them in his Catechism; he, then, gives his instruction concerning them.

> **"These are the most necessary parts of Christian instruction. We should learn to repeat them word for word. Our children should be taught the habit of reciting them daily when they rise in the morning, when they go to their meals, and when they go to bed at night."** (*Large Catechism*, P.7, par 15,16a).

Notice, "Luther, the Dictator," says they are to repeat all three at least three times a day. Then Luther tells what punishment should be given to children who cannot repeat all three, word for word. Let Luther speak for himself.

> **"Until they repeat them, they SHOULD NOT BE GIVEN ANYTHING TO EAT OR DRINK."** (*Large Catechism*, P.7, Par. #16b).

This is unbelievable! Here is a dictator in action. Has Luther taken away the rights of the parents to decide what portions of the Bible or what Scriptures they want their children to memorize? Do not the parents have the responsibility to decide what and if any punishment is to be rendered?

Now, as we continue in the Catechism, we go beyond "Luther, the Dictator" to another phase of Luther's philosophy, which is as I have said, "My way or the highway." In other words, if you are employed by Luther and do not believe the way he does, you are to be fired! Let us let Luther speak for himself.

> **"Every father has the same duty to his household; HE SHOULD DISMISS men-servants and maid-servants IF they do not know these things and are unwilling to learn them. Under no circumstances should a person be tolerated if he is so rude and unruly that he refuses to learn these THREE PARTS..."** (Large Catechism, P.7, Paragraphs 17, 18).

Martin Luther did not believe in religious freedom for all. He did not respect the rights and free will of others. He was a very hateful man, as he displayed towards the Jewish people.

He wanted employers to fire their employees if they refused to believe as he did. It is unthinkable that Luther would withhold food and water from children until they memorized, word for word, the three articles Luther listed.

Then, he lied about God's Ten Commandments, and this is the man Lutheran preachers pawn off to the unsuspecting public as a great theologian and liberator! This man was a tyrant, a dictator, and had no respect for the rights of others who disagreed with his religious philosophy.

Every Christian in America ought to be so thankful to God that Luther is not living today in America. He would be persuading the leaders here to persecute the Jews, just as he did those in power in Germany during the World War II years and before, by his writings.

No wonder Hitler loved Martin Luther and passed out his literature throughout Germany, as they both hated the Jewish people. The end result was the extermination of over six million people; men, women, and children. Since this hatred of the Jewish people came from a preacher, the German people believed it to be justified.

If Luther could be released out of the torments of Hades, I can only imagine him screaming at the top of his voice, "I was wrong! Baptism didn't save me and it will never save you. I should have loved the Jewish people, instead of hating and hurting them. I should have followed Paul's love and attitude as described in Romans 10:1."

> *"Brethren, my heart's desire and prayer to God for Israel is, that they might be saved."*

Chapter Nine

Luther's False Doctrine of Eschatology

There are four major areas of doctrine concerning the "end times" that Luther refused to believe. These four important doctrines include:

- ***The "Rapture" and the 7-Year Tribulation Period.*** The 7-Year Tribulation Period begins immediately following the Rapture of the Church, and is prophesied in Daniel 9:24-27. It is also known as the "70th Week of Daniel." The events described between Revelation, Chapters 4 and 19, take place during this 7 years of God's judgment upon the earth. This is all denied by Luther.

    ❖ ***The Rapture Explained:*** "The Rapture of the Church refers to the event which is prophesied in I Thessalonians 4:16,17,

    > *"For the Lord himself shall descend from heaven with a shout, with the voice of the archangel, and with the trump of God: and the dead in Christ shall rise first:"* (V.16).
    >
    > *"Then we which are alive and remain shall be caught up together with them in the clouds, to meet the Lord in the air: and so shall we ever be with the Lord."* (V.17).

This Scripture reveals that living Christians at the time of the Rapture "will be caught up," or raptured, with those resurrected to meet the Lord in the air. This event we know has not yet occurred, but it will be fulfilled in the near future. This same event is also described in I Corinthians 15:49-54, as well as many other places.

- ***The Restoration of the Jewish Nation.***

- ***The fulfillment of God's Promises to Abraham, Isaac, and Jacob.*** This is the literal rule and reign of Jesus Christ in the Kingdom on earth for 1,000 years.

In order to deny the literal fulfillment of the hundreds and hundreds of prophecies concerning these major doctrines, Luther fell into another trap door of Satan. He, therefore, spiritualized them; instead of believing that God would literally fulfill what He had predicted.

The Evangelical Lutheran Churches of America (ELCA); the Missouri Synod, and the Wisconsin Synod have, all three, followed their god, Martin Luther, in propagating the same false teaching.

- ***The Missouri Synod.***

In their booklet entitled "THE DOCTRINAL POSITION of the MISSOURI SYNOD," they state precisely what they reject concerning the Millennium (i.e., the 1,000-Year Kingdom Reign of Christ on earth as King of Kings and Lord of Lords).

a. "With the Augsburg Confession (Art. XVII). We reject every type of Millennialism." (P.19, Par. 42).

b. "Or Chiliasm," the opinion that Christ will return visibly to this earth a thousand years before the end of the world." (Ibid).

c. "Or that before the general resurrection on judgment day a number of departed Christians or Martyrs are to be raised again to reign in glory in this world." (Ibid). This is referring to their denial of the Rapture, as spoken of in I Thessalonians 4:13-17; I Corinthians 15:50-54, and many other places in the Bible.

d. Luther also did not believe: "That before the end of the world a universal conversion of the Jewish Nation (of Israel according the flesh) will take place." (P.20, 1st Par.).

Luther's hatred towards the Jews was so intense that it totally blinded him from believing God's promises concerning the Nation of Israel. He did not believe all the hundreds of Scriptures prophesying that Israel would be an established nation on earth and inherit all the land that God had promised to Abraham and his seed. (Genesis 13:1-17; 15:18-21; 17:7,8; Jeremiah 31:31-34). Ezekiel, Chapters 40-48, for example, describe in minute detail what transpires concerning Israel during the Thousand Year Reign of Christ, in His Kingdom on earth.

This was the same philosophy of the Roman Catholic church, which inherited it from Origen and Augustine (354-430 A.D.). This school of philosophy has been identified by different names; such as, "Amillennialism," "Replacement Theology," and "Covenant Theology," etc.

In other words, they spiritualize all the prophecies referring to Israel and the earthly Kingdom (the Millennium) and deny any literal fulfillment, as God has promised in the future.

Therefore, they take all the future promised blessings of God for Israel and "spiritually" transfer them to the church. They deny any literal fulfillment of God's promises to Israel. This same corrupt philosophy is alive and well today, thanks to Satan and his *"...false apostles, deceitful workers, transforming themselves into the apostles of Christ. And no marvel; for Satan himself is transformed into an angel of light."* (II Corinthians 11:13,14). Christ describes all false teachers in the same category with these in Matthew 23:27.

> *"Woe unto you, scribes and Pharisees, hypocrites! for ye are like unto whited sepulchres, which indeed appear beautiful outward, but are within full of dead men's bones, and of all uncleanness."*

To those I have talked with who advocate denying the Millennial Kingdom, I have proposed the following question to them: "Since you take it upon yourself to take all the ***prophetic blessings*** promised to Israel and spiritually apply them to the church; then, why do you not do the same with all other prophetic Scriptures, including the ***judgments?"***

For example, God prophesied that Israel would be taken captive by Assyria. Judah and Benjamin (the Southern Tribes) would be taken captive by Babylon. Then, Babylon would be taken by the Medo-Persians who, in turn, would fall to the Grecians, who would fall to the Roman Empire. These were prophesies of judgment against Israel and Judah and Benjamin. Why do you not spiritualize all the prophesies of *judgment* and apply them to the Church, just as you spiritualize all the *future blessings* and transfer them to the Church?

In reality, those following Martin Luther's philosophy, only spiritualize the Scriptures they want to, in order to make them fit their own preconceived ideas. The reason they didn't spiritualize the judgments on Israel is because they were already LITERALLY FULFILLED! Therefore, since God *literally* fulfilled His previous judgments as pronounced on Israel, *why* would God deviate from *literally* fulfilling His promised blessings of the Millennium upon Israel, which have never been fulfilled as yet?

God has some advice for these false teachers who pick and choose, using the Bible as a "Scripture Cafeteria," choosing what they want to believe and denying what they do not want to believe. Here is the Lord's advice as recorded in Isaiah 42:9,

> *"Behold, the former things are come to pass, and new things do I declare: before they spring forth I tell you of them."*

God further admonishes these false teachers, who deny any future Millennium, blessings or restoration of the Nation of Israel in Isaiah 48:3, on the basis of His past predictions and fulfillments.

> *"I have declared the former things from the beginning; and they went forth out of my mouth, and I shewed them; I did them suddenly, and they came to pass."*

Luther knew from Scripture and confirmation of History, that the judgments God had predicted upon Israel for their idolatry had been literally fulfilled. BUT, his hatred for the Jews blinded his eyes to the truth of God's Word which promised Israel's restoration in their own land when *"...all Israel shall be saved...."* (Romans 11:26a).

I would like to draw your attention to just a couple of the hundreds of Scriptures that speak of Israel's restoration in their own promised land. One passage is found in Ezekiel 36:24-28,

> *"For I will take you from among the heathen, and gather you out of all countries, and will bring you into your own land."*(V.24).

> *"Then will I sprinkle clean water upon you, and ye shall be clean: from all your filthiness, and from all your idols, will I cleanse you."*(V.25).

> *"A new heart also will I give you, and a new spirit will I put within you: and I will take away the stony heart out of your flesh, and I will give you an heart of flesh."*(V.26).

> *"And I will put my spirit within you, and cause you to walk in my statutes, and ye shall keep my judgments, and do them."*(V.27).

> *"And ye shall dwell in the land that I gave to your fathers; and ye shall be my people, and I will be your God."*(V.28).

The rest of Ezekiel 36, describes what transpires during the Millennial Reign of Christ on earth. Notice God's promise to Israel, and His blessing to them in Ezekiel 37:13,14.

> *"And ye shall know that I am the LORD, when I have opened your graves, O my people, and brought you up out of your graves,"* (V.13).

> *"And shall put my spirit in you, and ye shall live, and I shall place you in your own land: then shall ye know that I the LORD have spoken it, and performed it, saith the LORD."*(V.14).

Hear God's promise to Israel in Ezekiel 37:21-23.

> *"And say unto them, Thus saith the Lord GOD; Behold, I will take the children of Israel from among the heathen, whither they be gone, and will gather them on every side, and bring them into their own land:* (V.21).

> *And I will make them one nation in the land upon the mountains of Israel; and one king shall be king to them all: and they shall be no more two nations, neither shall they be divided into two kingdoms any more at all:* (V.22).

> *"Neither shall they defile themselves any more with their idols, nor with their detestable things, nor with any of their transgressions: but I will save them out of all their dwelling places, wherein they have sinned, and will cleanse them: so shall they be my people, and I will be their God."* (V.23).

Luther absolutely refused to believe in the future blessings that God had promised to Israel. God's Word, through the mouth of Isaiah, describes the unbelievers of Isaiah's day as well as those in the future, which includes Martin Luther. In Isaiah 48:6 we have the record.

> *"Thou hast heard, see all this; and will not ye declare it?..."*

Luther did not believe in Israel's future restoration; because, he never believed God's Word that it would ever take place. God describes Luther, as well as other false teachers who believe only what fits their own philosophy and humanistic reasoning.

> *"Because I knew that thou art obstinate, and thy neck is an iron sinew, and thy brow brass;"* (Isaiah 48:4).

I have only briefly inserted this information for our readers to acknowledge the origin of this false teaching of Amillennialism, Replacement Theology, and Covenant Theology. This idea of "no Millennium," to the best of my knowledge, first sprang up, as previously stated, in the Third Century and was taught by a man named Origen (185-254 A.D.) and endorsed by Augustine (354-430 A.D.) in the Fourth Century. The Roman Catholic Church practically worships Augustine and holds to his philosophy of "no Millennium." Luther, being raised in the Roman Church, and loving it, adapted the same philosophy.

After 460 some years, Luther's robot preachers are "programmed" or "brainwashed" through his colleges to propagate the same philosophy of denying all the Old Testament verses promising all these blessings on earth to Israel, during the Millennium.

If Martin Luther were living in America today, he would be relentless in trying to persuade our President to withdraw all aid and support for Israel. Luther's hatred of the Jewish people blinded him to the truth of God's words to Abraham in Genesis 12:3,

> *"And I will bless them that bless thee, and curse him that curseth thee: and in thee shall all families of the earth be blessed."* (Genesis 12:3).

Luther contributed to the curse of God on Germany, and he would do the same to America if he were living today!

I have inserted the following two diagrams, to illustrate how many of the biblical prophecies regarding the future, and their literal fulfillment, that Luther disregards and refuses to believe.

Diagram One, "True Biblical Eschatology;" and Diagram Two, "Martin Luther's Perverted Philosophy," follow on next two pages.

Diagram One
TRUE BIBLICAL ESCHATOLOGY

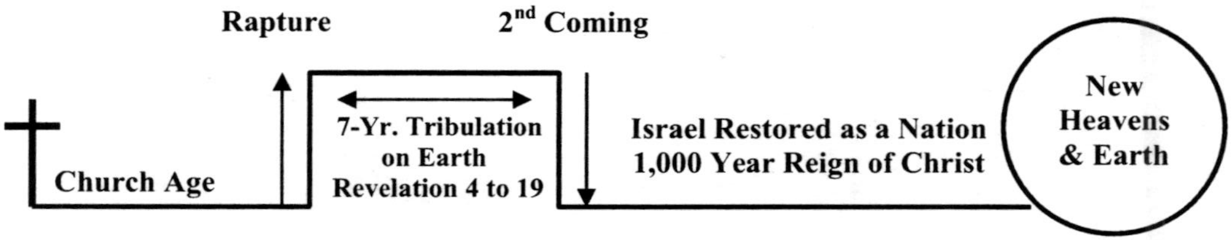

Explanation: This Diagram shows the Church Age, beginning after Calvary and concluding with the Rapture. Immediately following the Rapture begins seven literal years of God's judgment upon the earth, as described in Rev. 4:1 to Rev. 19:10, and known as the "7-Yr. Tribulation." The Tribulation Period ends at Christ's "2nd Coming. Christ returns to this earth, judges the nations; all Old Testament saved receive their resurrected bodies; and Israel, as a nation, will rule and reign with Christ for one thousand literal years (Rev. 19:11 to Rev. 20:4).

Diagram Two
MARTIN LUTHER'S PERVERTED PHILOSOPHY

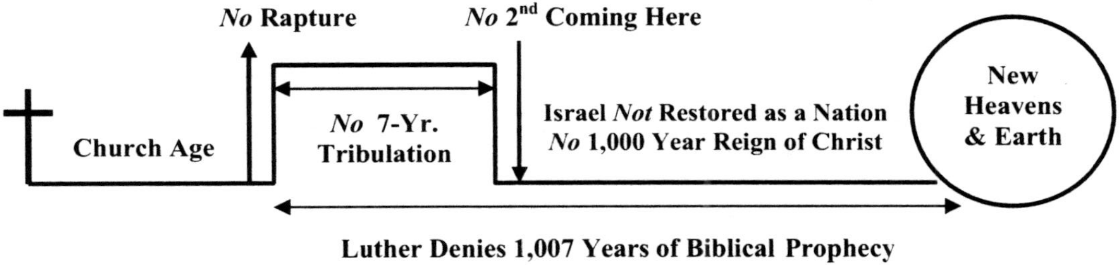

Explanation: This Diagram reveals Luther's philosophy which originated with Origen and Augustine in the Third and Fourth Century. The philosophy of Origen and Augustine was followed by the Roman Catholic organization and then adopted by Martin Luther and his followers. This denial of Scripture results in *no* Rapture, *no* 7-Yr. Tribulation, *no* fulfillment of God's Kingdom promises to Israel, and *no* Millennium, and *no* Thousand-Year Reign of Christ. These Doctrines are all clearly taught in Scripture. The result is, I have talked with myriads of Catholics and Lutherans, who have never heard of the Rapture or the Millennial Reign of Christ!

Diagram One illustrates the Church Age, which will conclude with the Rapture. Immediately following the Rapture begins the seven, literal years of God's judgment upon the earth as described in the Book of Revelation from Chapters 4 to 19. In Revelation 19, Christ returns to this earth, judges the nations; all Old Testament saved receive their resurrected bodies; and Israel, as a nation, will rule and reign with Christ for 1,000 literal years.

In Revelation 20, the length of the 1,000 years is stated 6 different times. This is what Luther denies. He denies the hundreds of Scriptures that describe in minute detail those prophecies which prove the events of Diagram One.

Diagram Two illustrates Luther's philosophy, which originated with Origen and Augustine in the 3rd and 4th Century. Their philosophy was followed by the Roman Catholic organization and adopted by Martin Luther and his followers. I have talked with myriads of Catholics and Lutherans who have never heard of the Rapture or the Millenial Reign of Christ.

For example, in Luther's Catechisms, you will find that when he speaks concerning the end of the Church Age, he states the Church Age will continue until Christ comes to judge mankind, and culminate in the creation of new heavens and earth. He, therefore, denies the Rapture, the 7-Year Tribulation Period, the Millennial Reign of Christ, and Israel restored as a nation. Here are a couple of Luther's references to substantiate this:

> **"Even as He calls, gathers, enlightens, and sanctifies the whole Christian church on earth, and keeps it with Jesus Christ in the one true faith;...and will at the *Last Day* raise up me and all the dead."** (*Small Catechism*, P.11, under "Sanctification.").

> **"He (Christ) descended into hell; the third day He rose again from the dead; He ascended into heaven, and sitteth on the right hand of God the Father Almighty; from thence *He shall come to judge the quick and the dead.*"** (*Small Catechism*, P. 10, under "Redemption.").

By the way, if you haven't noticed, Luther stated that Christ went to Hell. The "great theologian" must have overlooked Luke 23:43, which states that Christ went to Paradise, NOT Hell. Here is the record.

> *"And Jesus said unto him, Verily I say unto thee, To day shalt thou be with me in PARADISE."*

The foregoing is meant only to enlighten anyone, including Lutheran worshippers, as to what this man does *not* believe concerning God's Word. Should one be interested in an excellent, in-depth study concerning the Millenium, Amillenialism and the fallacies of Replacement Theology (also known as Covenant Theology), I would highly recommend the following book: *"The Millennial Kingdom"* by John F. Walvoord, Zondervan Publishing House, Grand Rapids, Michigan 49530

In Conclusion: Why is it important to believe what the Bible says about Eschatology, defined as "the Doctrine of Last Things;" or, in other words, future prophetic events such as the Rapture of the Church, the Tribulation, Restoration of Israel, and the Millennium?

- ❖ Because God said it! We should believe it!

  "... let God be true, but every man a liar;" (Romans 3:4).

- ❖ The Rapture of the Church is the "*Blessed Hope*" of the believer with which we are to *comfort one another.*

  "Looking for that blessed hope, and the glorious appearing of the great God and our Saviour Jesus Christ;" (Titus 2:13).

  "Then we (all saved) *which are alive and remain shall be caught up together with them* (the dead *in Christ) in the clouds, to meet the Lord in the air: and so shall we ever be with the Lord.* (V.17).

  Wherefore comfort one another with these words." (I Thessalonians 4:17,18).

- ❖ The Restoration of the Nation of Israel and the return to their land (All of it!) in the Millennium are *precious promises of God to the Jewish people.*

- ❖ Believing that *God is never going to fail* in the fulfillment of his covenant promises to Abraham,

Isaac, and Jacob, and their children, the Nation of Israel, *results in a right attitude* toward the Jewish people of today. We will then be able to say, as did the Apostle Paul,

"Brethren, my heart's desire and prayer to God for Israel is, that they might be saved." (Romans 10:1).

❖ *God will bless us* for loving his "chosen people," the Jews.

"Pray for the peace of Jerusalem: they shall prosper that love thee." (Psalm 122:6).

"And I will bless them that bless thee, and curse him that curseth thee: and in thee shall all families of the earth be blessed." (Genesis 12:3).

What are you going to do? Starve yourself at Martin Luther's "Scripture Cafeteria;" or feast at God's banquet table of precious promises?

"And they said, Believe on the Lord Jesus Christ, and thou shalt be saved,..." (Acts 16:31).

Chapter Ten

Martin Luther's False Views of God's Word

- ***Revealed by the Epistles Luther Rejected as Uncanonical: Hebrews, James, Jude, Revelation.***

Of the 27 books of the New Testament, all were written by the end of the 1st Century A.D. There were translations into other languages and they became spread throughout, as well as expositions and commentaries.

The churches, in general, were practically unanimous as to the authenticity and canonicity of our 27 books, excluding all other writings before the end of the 4th Century. In 382 A.D., the Council of Damascus at Rome considered the 27 New Testament books complete. In 393 A.D., the Councils of Hippo were like-minded. The Councils of Carthage (397 A.D. and 419 A.D.) concluded the same. For a thousand years, practically all the churches, East and West, down to the Reformation and the Council of Trent (1546 A.D.), were of the same opinion.

Did Martin Luther agree? NO! Luther could never reconcile the book of James with the book of Romans; as, they seemed to contradict each other. This baffled and confused Luther! For example, Romans 4:5 and James 2:17 seemed to be at odds with each other.

> *"Even so faith, if it hath not works, is dead, being alone."* (James 2:17).

> *"But to him that worketh not, but believeth on him that justifieth the ungodly, his faith is counted for righteousness."* (Romans 4:5).

Luther, the great, so-called scholar and theologian, was unable to discern a very simple truth concerning Romans and James. He could not see that Romans is presenting a POSITIONAL truth; i.e., JUSTIFICATION IN GOD'S EYES. In other words, Salvation is a free gift (Ephesians 2:8,9), exempting any kind of works, *including baptism*!

Further, James is presenting a PRACITICAL truth concerning our WALK, or behavior after we become a Christian; therefore JUSTIFICATION in man's eyes.

Therefore, if I witness to someone about Christ and Salvation, and that person knows that I am living a despicable life, my witnessing will fall on *dead ears*. If my life does not show what a person expects to see in a Christian's life; therefore, my *"faith...is dead"* when witnessing to someone else.

Anything Luther didn't understand and thought to be contradictory to his beliefs, he regarded as un-apostolic, unauthoritative, and practically uncanonical. He, therefore, placed Hebrews, James, Jude, and Revelation at the end of his New Testament as uncanonical. Also, in his Table of Contents they are separated from the other books and un-numbered in his German Translation (1521-1522 A.D.).

- ***Luther claimed that Christ ascended to Heaven in His human nature!***

In *Luther's Small Catechism*, P.118, #153, entitled,

"What do the scriptures teach of Christ's ascension into Heaven?"

"The Scriptures teach that, according to His *HUMAN* NATURE, Christ *visibly* ascended to heaven and entered *into the glory* of His Father, as our *Forerunner.* Hebrews 6:20."

NOT TRUE! Christ, after His death, three days later arose from the dead in his RESURRECTED BODY (I Corinthians 15:3,4). He walked on this earth 40 days, as Acts 1:3 states:

> *"To whom also he shewed himself alive after his passion* (His death on the cross, then resurrected) *by many infallible proofs, being seen of them forty days, and speaking of the things pertaining to the kingdom of God:"*

In appearance, Christ's resurrected and glorified body was essentially identical with His earthly body that came forth from Mary's womb. Notice the words of Christ in Luke 24...

> *"And he said unto them, Why are ye troubled? and why do thoughts arise in your hearts?*(V.38).

> *Behold my hands and my feet, that it is I myself: handle me, and see; for a spirit hath not flesh and bones, as ye see me have."* (Luke 24:38-39).

Notice carefully that Christ states that His resurrected body is composed of flesh and BONES; not flesh and BLOOD. This is very important, because the Christians resurrected bodies are going to be like Christ's resurrected body. Notice in Philippians, Chapter Three.

> *For our conversation* (Gr. meaning "heavenly citizenship") *is in heaven; from whence also we look for the Saviour, the Lord Jesus Christ:*
>
> *Who shall change our vile body, that it may be fashioned like unto his glorious body, according to the working whereby he is able even to subdue all things unto himself."* (Philippians 3:20-21).

Therefore, when the Christian inherits his citizenship in Heaven, the earthly body of a Christian will be changed into a resurrected body *like* the glorified, resurrected body of Christ. God's Word clearly declares this in I Corinthians, Chapter 15 that...

> *"Now this I say, brethren, that flesh and blood cannot inherit the kingdom of God; neither doth corruption inherit incorruption."* (I Corinthians 15:50).

We know from the foregoing Scriptures that Christ's earthly body was not just brought back to life as the same body He had preceding His death. His resurrected body was void of any blood, such as His earthly body possessed.

Therefore, Christ's resurrected body was composed of flesh and bone, entirely foreign to our human bodies, which contain blood. As a Christian and a citizen of Heaven, we will reign with Christ in our new, glorified body with God's promise and assurance that...

> *"And God shall wipe away all tears from their eyes; and there shall be no more death, neither sorrow, nor crying, neither shall there be any more pain: for the former things are passed away."* (Revelation 21:4).

In our resurrected bodies, we will never experience again the things we experienced in our earthly bodies while on earth.

Luther's claim that Christ ascended to Heaven according to his Human Nature, would have Christ raised from the dead with the same body of flesh and blood that He was buried in. This would mean that the body of a Christian, since it is fashioned after Christ's resurrected body, would also be resurrected as the same corruptible body that had died. (We would be like Lazarus, raised from the dead, only to die again at a later time.) This is absolutely impossible! Revelation 21:4 states that all the things we experienced in our earthly bodies, we will *never* experience in our resurrected bodies in our Heavenly home.

Who are you going to believe? The infallible Word of God or the Catechism written by Luther, the "Master of Deceit."

- ***Luther claims that Christ descended into Hell.***

The following are Martin Luther's own words as found in his *Small Catechism* on P.116, Section #150.

> **"150. What do the Scriptures teach of Christ's descent into hell?**
>
> **The Scriptures teach that Christ, having been *made alive* in His grave, descended into hell, not to suffer, but to *proclaim His victory over His enemies.***
>
> **[Christ was] put to death in the flesh, but quickened by the spirit; by which also *He went and preached* unto the spirits in prison. *I Peter 3:18,19.*"**

It is not my intention to write a full exposition on Luther's false theological beliefs contained in the above statement. I am only going to point out the errors that contradict other Scriptures with brief comments.

- ***First Error:*** "Christ having been *made alive* in His grave." Christ was never "made alive" in the grave, as Christ never died and went to the grave. The body gave up the Spirit, i.e., Christ, who was manifested in the flesh could never die, only the body. You cannot "kill God!"

- ***Second Error:*** Christ "descended into Hell." This is unbelievable, as this would contradict the clear statement of Christ, Himself, in Luke 23:43! Here,

Jesus is speaking in Verse 42 to the "Thief on The Cross," who is now saved.

"And Jesus said unto him, Verily I say unto thee, To day shalt thou be with me in paradise." (Luke 23:43).

- ***Third Error:*** "*Also, He* (i.e., Christ) *went and preached unto the spirits in prison."* (I Peter 3:19). Luther should have also quoted I Peter 3:20, which gives the *context* of Verse 19; but, failed to do so as it would contradict his teaching.

Now let us see what God is really saying, when we read Verses 19 and 20 together.

"By which also he (Christ) *went and preached unto the spirits in prison;* (V.19).

Which sometime were disobedient, when once the longsuffering of God waited (Genesis 6:3, for 120 years) *in the days of Noah, while the ark was a preparing, wherein few, that is, eight souls were saved by* ("through") *water."* (I Peter 3:19-20).

Very simply, these verses teach that Christ preached through Noah just as He does today through Christians who proclaim His Word to the lost, just as Noah did in the days before the flood. The people of Noah's day were imprisoned in their sin as,

"... every imagination of the thoughts of his heart was only evil continually." (Genesis 6:5b).

God waited 120 years, then sent the flood judgment. Only eight people were saved in the ark, which carried them through the destroying flood waters. A far cry from Luther omitting I Peter 3:20, which explains Verse 19, so he can lead you to believe that Christ went to a literal Hell where the lost are held. Christ did not go to "Hell," He went to Paradise! Please note Acts 2:31, which states,

> *"He seeing this before spake of the resurrection of Christ, that his soul was not left in* <u>HELL</u> (Gr. "hades"), *neither his flesh did see corruption."* (Acts 2:31).

Read Luke 16:19-31. The word *"hell"* here is the same Greek word "hades." It had two compartments, one for the lost and one for the saved, separated by a great gulf. In Verses 22,23, the lost man was in torment and the beggar, who was saved, went to a place within Hades called "Abraham's Bosom." This is where Christ went, which He called "Paradise" in Luke 23:43.

For a detailed study of Hell, with many diagrams, get our book entitled *"A Biblical Examination of Hell."*

Here is Luther, again, stating and leading one to believe that Christ went to Hell for three days while His body was in the grave. This is totally foreign to the Bible! He honestly has earned the title he deserves, "the Master of Deceit," by extracting one verse completely out of context to fit his preconceived philosophy.

Remember, Luther knew the Greek as he translated from it into his German Bible. Yet, his preachers today pawn off his false teachings by distributing his Catechisms to their unsuspecting church members.

Has your Lutheran preacher made known to you these lies concerning Luther's so-called Theology. If not, WHY? One would have to conclude they must believe the same false teaching as Martin Luther propagates which, in turn, they indoctrinate you with. Christ in addressing the false teachers of His day, which is applicable to all false teachers, states in Mark, Chapter Seven, the following.

> *"Howbeit in vain* (Gr. "emptiness") *do they worship me, teaching for doctrines the commandments of men."* (Mark 7:7).

Chapter Eleven

False Teachings of Martin Luther Concerning Faith and Salvation.

- ***Faith has to be in something visible!***

Luther believes that faith has to be in something visible, something you can see; something MORE than the death, burial and resurrection of Jesus Christ as recorded in God's written word, the Bible. As unbelievable as this is, here are Luther's own words in his Catechism:

> **"But these leaders of the blind are unwilling to see that FAITH must have something to believe—something to which it may cling and upon which it may stand. Thus FAITH CLINGS TO THE WATER and believes it to be baptism in which there is sheer Salvation and life..."** (*Large Catechism*, P. 84, Par. 29).

The last words of Christ upon the cross, when He died in payment for the sins of every human being were, "IT IS FINISHED." Here is the record from Christ, Himself,

> *"When Jesus therefore had received the vinegar, he said, <u>It is finished</u>: and he bowed his head, and gave up the ghost."* (John 19:30).

Christ stated, "*It is finished*" and nothing further could be done or added beyond. Nothing but just simple FAITH IN JESUS CHRIST'S finished payment for our sins would ever be accepted for eternal life. How many times have you heard preachers and layman quote Luther as saying, "The just shall live by faith." This is very deceitful, as Luther *never* trusted in the *finished* work of Christ on the cross for his salvation. Notice Luther's claim that...

> **"...FAITH must have something to believe—something to which it may cling and upon which it may stand..."**

Since Martin Luther did not come on the scene until about 1500 years after Christ, he did not witness the death, burial and resurrection of Christ. Therefore, Luther's definition of faith has to be in something he can observe. Evidently, Luther did not put much credibility in the "Great Faith Chapter" of Hebrews, Chapter 11.This chapter describes the great faith of many who believed God's promises before they ever saw any evidence. The first verse of Hebrews, Chapter 11, is the introduction to the rest of the chapter.

> *"Now faith is the substance of things hoped for, the evidence of things not seen."* (Hebrews 11:1).

Luther really did not believe Hebrews 11:1. This is why he did not believe Christ's words on the cross, "IT IS FINISHED," because he wasn't there to see it for himself! Luther's faith rested in what he could *do* and *observe.* Here is Luther's testimony as recorded in his Catechism.

> **"Thus faith clings to the *water* and believes it to be *Baptism* in which there is sheer *salvation* and life..."** (*Large Catechism*, P.84, Par. 29).

The true Christian opposes the above philosophy of Luther, as their faith is in Jesus Christ and His *finished* work on Calvary which provided for their Salvation. Our faith is in the Bible; NOT in the writings of a Catechism, written some 460 years ago.

Here is the confidence the Christian has:

> *"He that believeth on the Son of God hath the witness in himself:.."* (V.10a).

> *"And this is the record, that God hath given to us eternal life, and this life is in his Son."*(V.11).

> *"He that hath the Son hath life; and he that hath not the Son of God hath not life."*(V.12).

> *"These things have I written unto you that believe on the name of the Son of God; that ye may know that ye have eternal life, and that ye may believe on the name of the Son of God."* (I John 5:10a-13).

In conclusion, notice carefully the distinction between God's Word, the Bible, and Luther's words in his Catechism.

- ***God's Word***, in I John 5:10-13 it states plainly that "belief" in Jesus Christ, the Son of God gives eternal life. No baptism in any of these verses.

- ***Luther's Belief***, as he proclaimed in his *Large Catechism*, Page 84, Par. 29, disagree with God's Word.

> **FAITH must have something to believe—something to which it may cling and upon which it may stand.**

Luther says that those who disagree with him are the "leaders of the blind."

- ***God answers*** Luther's false claim,

> *"...he that believeth not God hath made him a liar; because he believeth not the record that God gave of his Son."* (I John 5:10b).

"It is finished," said Jesus Christ in John 19:30. Since the Word of God is true, the only alternative is that Martin Luther is the "leader of the blind," not Jesus Christ.

> **Luther states that, without the two sacraments (i.e. Baptism and the Lord's Supper, no one can be a Christian.** (*Large Catechism*, P.80).

Luther states in his *Small Catechism* on Page 169, Paragraph 243 that,

> **"There are only two such Sacraments, Holy Baptism and the Lord's Supper."**

(Luther prolifically uses the word "holy" with "baptism. Such a statement is found nowhere in the Bible!) In Paragraph 242 of Page 169, Luther says that,

> **"By a sacrament we mean a sacred act. By which God offers, gives, and seals unto us THE FORGIVENESS OF SINS which Christ has earned for us."**

Now, in Luther's *Large Catechism*, Page 80, under "Baptism, Paragraph 1," he states that,

> **"...because without these (i.e. Baptism and the Passover Feast) no one can be a Christian."**

Does Luther really know what he believes? In his Large and *Small Catechisms*, he repeatedly states that he believes baptism saves you and effects forgiveness of sins. Here are his words.

- ***Small Catechism*** – under **"What does Baptism give or profit?**

  "It works forgiveness of sins, delivers from death and the devil, and gives eternal salvation to all who believe this, as the

words and promises of God declare." (P.174, II).

- ***Large Catechism*** – (P.83, Par. 24).

"To put it most simply, the power, effect, benefit, fruit, and purpose of Baptism is to save. To be saved, we know, is nothing else than to be delivered from sin, death, and the devil, and to enter into the kingdom of Christ and live with him forever."

- ***The Contradiction*** - Now Luther contradicts himself and states that you cannot be a Christian unless you ALSO partake of another sacrament; i.e. THE LORD'S SUPPER. Here are Luther's own words.

"It remains for us to speak of our two sacraments,...because without these NO ONE CAN BE A CHRISTIAN. (*Large Catechism*, P. 80, Par. 1).

Luther continued in his *Large Catechism* and states plainly that he believes a person obtains the forgiveness of sins by *partaking* of the Passover Feast, known as The Last Supper, before Christ went to the cross, as recorded in Matthew, Chapter 26.

Here are Luther's words as he describes what he *thinks* he believes.

"We have briefly considered the first part, namely, the essence of this sacrament. Now

> **we come to its *power* and *benefit*, the purpose for which the sacrament was really instituted, for it is most necessary that we know what we should *seek* and *obtain* there. This is plainly evident from the words just quoted, "This is my body and blood, given and poured out for you for the *forgiveness of sins.*" In other words, we go to the Sacrament because we receive there great treasure, through and in which we obtain the *forgiveness of sins.*"** (*Luther's Large Catechism*, P. 93, Par. 20-22).

Luther is here referring to the Passover Feast in Matthew 26, which took place prior to Christ's going to the cross. This feast was first established in Exodus, Chapter 12, and would be in effect until Christ's crucifixion. One must remember that Matthew, Mark, Luke and John are primarily a continuation of the Old Covenant and the blood sacrifices, until the New Covenant was officiated by Christ upon Calvary. We know this was the Passover, because it is so stated by Christ, Himself, in Luke 22:13; Matthew 26:19; and Mark 14:14.

> *"And they went, and found as he had said unto them: and they made ready the PASSOVER."* (Luke 22:13).

Luther wants you to believe that when you partake of the Passover Feast, you receive forgiveness of your sins the same as you did when you were baptized. Remember, in *Luther's Large Catechism*, Page 80, he states that, **"...because without these** (i.e., baptism and the Passover Feast) **no one can be a Christian."**

In James 1:8 we are told that:

> *"A double minded man is unstable in all his ways."* (James 1:8).

First, Luther states in his *Small Catechism*, Page 174, II, that baptism forgives your sins and gives eternal salvation. Then, Luther, in his *Large Catechism*, Page 80, Par. 1, states that you cannot be a Christian unless you also partake of the Passover Feast, in which you receive forgiveness of sins. (*Large Catechism*, P. 93, Par. 20-22).

First, Baptism, then the Passover Feast, and now it takes two works of the flesh in order to obtain forgiveness of your sins and become a Christian. This is according to Martin Luther. Remember Luther's words in his Catechism!

> **"It remains for us to speak of our two sacraments,** (i.e., Baptism and the Last Passover Supper)**...because without these NO ONE CAN BE A CHRISTIAN."** (*Large Catechism*, P. 80, Par. 1).

Luther *did not* believe in the finished work of Christ on the cross for Salvation. He believed that Christ *purchased for us* eternal life and other blessings; BUT, they are only given to a person when they are baptized and partake of the Lord's Supper, "in which is the forgiveness of sins," according to Luther's own words.

Christ makes Luther out to be a liar and a false teacher, as He declares in John 14:6,

"Jesus saith unto him, I am the way, the truth, and the life: no man cometh unto the Father, but by me."
(John 14:6).

- ***Examination of Matthew 26:26-28.***

Now let us return to Luther's Catechism where he is referring to Matthew 26:28.

> **"This is my body and blood, given and poured out *for you* for the FORGIVENESS OF SINS." In other words, we go to the Sacrament because we receive there a great treasure, through and in which we OB-TAIN THE FORGIVENESS OF SINS."** (*Large Catechism*, P. 93, Par. 21,22).

> *"For this is my blood of the new testament, which is shed for many for the remission of sins."* (Matthew 26:28 from the Bible).

You will notice that Luther did not quote Verse 28 from the Bible correctly.

I would like to point out Jesus uses the broken bread to represent His body and the "*fruit of the vine*," as stated in Verse 29, to represent His blood that was to be shed. The "*fruit of the vine*" was always the sweet, unfermented grape juice; never alcoholic. The reason the Passover lamb was not used was that it pointed to Christ, Himself. It was a type of Christ: innocent, perfect, and unblemished. (I Peter 1:18,19). Since Christ was here in person, fulfilling the typology of the Lamb, there was no need for that sacrifice any more. John states in 1:29,

> *"The next day John seeth Jesus coming unto him, and saith, Behold the Lamb of God, which taketh away the sin of the world."*

Therefore the bread and "*fruit of the vine*" would be used to represent Christ's finished work of the cross for Salvation. Let us examine Matthew 26:26-28. Here is the record,

> *"And as they were eating, Jesus took bread, and blessed it, and brake it, and gave it to the disciples, and said, Take, eat; this is my body.* (V.26).
>
> *And he took the cup, and gave thanks, and gave it to them, saying, Drink ye all of it;* (V.27).
>
> *For this is my blood of the new testament, which is shed for many for the remission of sins."* (V.28).

I would like to look at each verse, separately, to observe the very simple truth that Christ is illustrating:

- ***Verse 26.***

Notice that Christ took the BREAD and broke it and said, "*Take eat, this is my body.*" In other words, this bread, being broken would represent His body on the cross. Christ was in His sinless body, as was represented by the literal unfermented bread. The body of Christ never turned into the bread; and, the bread never possessed or turned into the body of Christ. How could one literally eat the bread and say it was somehow turned into the literal flesh of Christ while He was alive in His body? The Bible never teaches such an absurdity!

This is called Transubstantiation, a belief held by the Catholic organization, who indwelt Luther with their philosophy. Luther, in turn, passed it on to his puppet preachers via the Catechisms. I have asked hundreds, and have never found a priest or a "Luther-ite" who said the bread tasted like human flesh!

- ***Luther's perversion of Matthew 26:26***. He states what he means in his *Large Catechism*.

> **"How can bread and wine be Christ's body and blood?"** (*Large Catechism*, P.92, Par.12).

Luther, and the Catholic organization, believe that when the priest or minister says, concerning the bread, "Take, eat, this is my body," that it actually turns into the literal flesh of Christ. Here are Luther's own words.

> **"It is true, indeed, that if you take the word away from the elements or view them apart from the word, you have nothing but ordinary bread and wine. BUT, if the words remain, as is right and necessary, then in virtue of them they are THE BODY AND BLOOD OF CHRIST."** (*Large Catechism*, P.92, Par. 14).

> **"But of that bread and wine which ARE CHRIST'S BODY AND BLOOD and with which the words are coupled."** (*Large Catechism,* P. 93, Par. 28).

Then, as usual, Luther contradicts himself! In his *Small Catechism,* P. 196, Par. 301, we read:

> **"Bread and wine are NOT CHANGED into the BODY AND BLOOD OF CHRIST..."**

Luther doesn't seem to know what he believes. In his *Large Catechism* he says that the bread and wine are just ordinary until God's word is connected to them; then, they are the body and blood of Christ. Then in his *Small Catechism* he says the bread and wine are *not* changed into Christ's body. Does Luther know *what* he believes? He states one thing one place and something different in another place.

All Luther has to do to prove himself right, along with his preachers today, is the following:

1. Ask any honest person who puts the wafer or bread in their mouth whether it tasted like bread, cracker, or human flesh, AFTER the preacher says his "miracle changing words," "Take, eat, this is my body."

2. My second test would be, open your mouth before you swallow, but AFTER the preacher's words, and I want to see if that wafer is still a wafer; or, if it has been turned into the flesh of Jesus' sinless body.

3. How could the bread be turned into the flesh of Jesus' body, when that body no longer exists? Jesus is now in His resurrected body, *after* His resurrection.

❖ ***Verse 27.***

In this verse, Christ took the cup, filled it with the sweet grape juice (*"fruit of the vine")* and gave it to His disciples to drink.

❖ ***Verse 28.*** In Verse 28, Christ states,

> *"For this is my blood of the new testament* (i.e., covenant), *which is shed for many for the remission of sins."*

Christ speaks as though His death on the cross had already taken place. Notice carefully the words, "my blood...which *is shed."* Here Christ speaks as though the future of the cross has already come to pass!

There is no forgiveness of sins in the act of baptism or the act of taking the Lord's Supper. These only represent what Christ did for us on the cross. There is no Salvation in the symbols and ordinances; but, only in the true substance itself. That is the death, burial, and resurrection of Jesus Christ, Himself.

Christ many times in the New Testament speaks as though the future has already been fulfilled. For example, in the high priestly prayer of Christ in John 17:4, He states,

> *"I have glorified thee on the earth: I have finished the work which thou gavest me to do."*

He had not gone to the cross yet; but, He was speaking as though it was already accomplished. Also in John 17:11a, Christ states,

> *"And now I am no more in the world..."*

Christ had not yet been crucified, resurrected three days later, and then walked 40 days on the earth prior to His ascension in Acts 1:11. But Christ was speaking as though all this had been fulfilled, including His ascension.

Conclusion: Luther was never a saved man, as his faith was not in Christ's last words on the cross, *"It is finished."* Luther's own writings condemn him, as he is not walking by faith *only* in Christ's payment for sin on the cross. Luther by his own admission walked by sight, as he had to see something that he had done to procure salvation. Here is his own testimony,

> **"Faith must have something to believe—something to which it may cling and upon which it may stand. Thus faith clings to the water and believes it to be baptism in which there is sheer Salvation and life."** (*Large Catechism*, P.84, Par. 29).

- ***The Scriptures Expose The Truth.***

The Word of God refutes and exposes Martin Luther as the "Master of Deceit" that he is. We have *"redemption through his* (Christ's) *blood.*" and so the following Scriptures declare:

1. **Ephesians 1:7**. *"In whom we have redemption through his blood, the forgiveness of sins, according to the riches of his grace; "*

2. **Romans 5:9**. *"Much more then, being now justified by his blood, we shall be saved from wrath through him."*

3. **Colossians 1:20a**. *"And, having made peace through the blood of his cross, by him* (Christ*) to reconcile all things unto himself;..."*

4. **Revelation 1:5b**. *"...Unto him* (Christ) *that loved us, and washed us from our sins in his own blood,"*

5. **Revelation 5:9b**. *"...and hast redeemed us to God by thy blood out of every kindred, and tongue, and people, and nation;"*

6. **Revelation 7:14.** *"...These are they which came out of great tribulation, and have washed their robes, and made them white in the blood of the Lamb."*

7. **Hebrews 9:22.** *"And almost all things are by the law purged with blood; and without shedding of blood is no remission."*

The *substance* of our faith is what Christ did on the cross by giving His life and shedding His blood as payment for the sins of all mankind. The *ordinance* concerning the Lord's Supper was given to the church, i.e., every saved person, to partake of as a *reminder* of what Christ did for them on the cross. This is recorded in I Corinthians 11:23-26.

> *"... That the Lord Jesus the same night in which he was betrayed took bread: And when he had given thanks, he brake it, and said, Take, eat: this is my body, which is broken for you: this do in remembrance of me."* (I Corinthians 11:23b,24).

> *"After the same manner also he took the cup, when he had supped, saying, This cup is the new testament in my blood: this do ye, as oft as ye drink it, in remembrance of me."* (I Corinthians 11:25).

> *"For as often as ye eat this bread, and drink this cup, ye do shew the Lord's death till he come."* (I Corinthians 11:26).

There is no salvation or forgiveness of sins in partaking of the Lord's Supper. It was given only to keep Christians aware and in constant REMEMBRANCE of what Christ did in order to provide for their Salvation; AND, remind them to look for His *coming again,* as stated in Verse 26.

Luther's faith was never in the finished work of Christ. His faith was in what he could *see and do,* i.e., the ordinances of Baptism and partaking of the Lord's Supper. Don't ever forget Luther's false claim in his *Large Catechism*, Page 84, Par. 29.

> **"FAITH must have something to believe—something to which it may cling and upon**

> **which it may stand. Thus faith clings to the WATER and believes it to be BAPTISM in which there is sheer SALVATION and life..."**

For the Christian, their faith is in the finished payment Christ made on the cross, providing salvation to all who would put their faith in Him, and Him alone.

> *"For by grace are ye saved through faith; and that not of yourselves: it is the gift of God: Not of works, lest any man should boast."* (Ephesians 2:8-9).

It is your choice. Should you choose to believe the "Master of Deceit" Luther, and his Catechisms, the end result is eternal damnation. (John 3:36b). Should you choose to believe Jesus Christ and the Word of God, the end result is eternal life. (John 3:36a). You are responsible for your own destiny!

Chapter Twelve

Satan's Big Lie: All Non-Catholics are Protestant

- ***The lie, that all non-Catholics are Protestants...***

...has been fostered by Satan throughout the world, and he continues to deceive people into believing this lie. We are told in God's Word that Satan is a murderer and a liar.

> *Ye are of your father the devil, and the lusts of your father ye will do. He was a murderer from the beginning, and abode not in the truth, because there is no truth in him. When he speaketh a lie, he speaketh of his own: for he is a liar, and the father of it."* (John 8:44).

Through out America, and parts of the world, Satan has people identified as belonging to one of three religious groups. Therefore, if you are not a Catholic, or a Jew, then all others are classified as Protestant. If this were true, then all denominations, churches, and religious groups would be classified as Protestant. This would then include all religions, such as Mormons, Scientology, Jehovah's Witnesses, Armstrongism, Unity School of Christianity, Lutherans, Baptist, Methodists, Episcopalians, Church of Christ, Pentecostal, and on, and on we go!

Nothing could be further from the truth. The reason Satan loves this lie is because he wants you to believe that the Roman Catholic organization, saturated with its false teachings, is really the Universal Church. Anyone who does not endorse their teachings is "anathema" (i.e., accursed) and in PROTEST; therefore, labeled as Protestants. In verification of this, their Catechism states on Page 48, Par. 181, that "No one can have God as Father who does not have the Church as Mother." This is another of Satan's lies, found nowhere in the Bible.

- ***Where did the word "Protestant" first come into existence? And who were the Protestants?***

We are going to see that ONLY those who were part of the Roman Catholic organization, but in protest of their teachings and withdrew or were excommunicated, were called Protestants.

On October 31, 1517, Luther, at the age of 33, nailed his 95 Theses on the door the castle church, located in Wittenberg, Germany. His main opposition was that the Catholic Church was selling indulgences for their sins to be forgiven.

In the early part of 1517, a man by the name of Johann Tetzel had begun selling indulgences on the border of Saxony. Among his "customers" were some of Luther's parishioners. Luther noticed that fewer people were coming to confession.

Luther believed the priest, as well as himself and his preachers, could forgive your sins, as he states in his *Small Catechism* on Page 188:

"CONFESSION AND ABSOLUTION:

> ***What is confession?* Confession embraces two parts. One is that we confess our sins; the other, that we receive absolution, or forgiveness, from the pastor AS FROM GOD HIMSELF, and in no wise doubt, but firmly believe, that by it our sins are forgiven before God in heaven."**

What Luther *opposed* was the people having to pay for this "forgiveness." This is what prompted him to nail his 95 Theses on the church door.

Twelve years later, after Luther posted his 95 Theses on the door of the castle church in Wittenberg, an important council was called; little recognized; but, of the utmost importance in History.

In 1529, February 21 through April 22, the Second Diet (i.e., Council) of Speyer was held. This was a Roman Catholic Council, convened for the purpose of taking action against Luther and his followers, and others who were not cooperating with the Pope and in protest of some of the church's teachings.

Several Lutheran princes appeared before this Roman Catholic Council with a formal written protest against those teachings which, in their opinion went contrary to their faith. This protest was signed by: Elector John of Saxony; Margrave George of Brandenberg; Dukes Ernest and Francis Braunschweig-Luneburg; Landgrave Philip of Hesse; Prince Wolfgang of Anhalt, and the representatives of fourteen (14) imperial cities. The protest was designed to protect them from the decisions of the Council.

Philip Schaaf, a great church historian stated in his *History of the Christian Church,* Vol.VII, P.692, the following:

> "From this protest and appeal, the ***Lutherans*** were called PROTESTANTS."

It was also originally used of those German princes and free cities who declared their opposition to the decision of the Diet (i.e., Council) of Speyer, which denounced their reformation and opposition to the Pope and Catholic teachings.

One can easily see the origin of the word "protestant" as it was first applied in the Sixteenth Century. They are Lutherans, the Reformed and others, who were ***once*** Roman Catholics and left the Roman Catholic organization and its false teachings to start denominations of their own, as did Martin Luther.

The word "Protestant" did not come into existence until the 16th Century. Prior to this, there were no Protestants, as the word was non-existent.

Those trusting Jesus Christ as their Savior, plus nothing, are called Christians from the time of Christ until the Rapture. They, along with the apostles, Paul, Peter, James, John; Timothy, Titus, Apollos, Priscilla and Aquila, and all the saved in the New Testament; those in Corinth,

Ephesus, Galatia, and etc., never bore the name of Protestant. They were just plain Christians.!

As time progressed, from the Council of Speyer in 1529 to the present, the name of Protestant has been applied to anyone who is not a Roman Catholic. Satan loves this idea as people, in general, have their minds implanted with the idea and claims of the Roman Catholic Church that they are the only true, universal church of all. Therefore, all others are just "protestants;" but, not of the true faith. How deceiving this is!

The Word of God tells us what the Universal Church is, who it is composed of and who is the Head. Every person who has accepted Jesus Christ, and Him alone, as their personal Savior has been placed into the spiritual Body of Christ. I Corinthians 12:13 makes this perfectly clear.

> *"For by one Spirit are we all baptized into one body, whether we be Jews or Gentiles, whether we be bond or free; and have been all made to drink into one Spirit."* (I Corinthians 12:13).

The HEAD of this universal body of Christians is Jesus Christ, NOT the Pope, Cardinals, nor his so-called priests. Ephesians 5:23 states,

> *"...Christ is the head of the church: and he is the saviour of the body."* (Not the Pope!) (Ephesians 5:23b).

Ephesians 5:24a states that a Christian's allegiance is to Christ.

> *"Therefore as the church* (every Christian) *is subject unto Christ,..."* (Not the Pope!)

Ephesians 5:25 lets us know, of a certainty, that it was Jesus Christ who gave Himself for the church on the cross; followed by His death and resurrection, so that every believer would make up the Body of Christ.

> *"Husbands, love your wives, even as Christ also loved the church, and gave himself for it;* (Not the Pope!)

I could write a volume of pages in continuation of this subject; but, that is not my purpose at this time. I have only inserted this brief coverage to give people a little information about the word "protestant," which is so misused and misunderstood.

Personally, I am now speaking of myself. My faith is in the payment Christ made for me on the cross. Christ's last words on the cross in John 19:30 were, "*It is finished.*" My faith is in Jesus Christ, and Him alone, who paid for my sins on the cross; therefore, ***I know*** I possess eternal life. John 3:16 is my assurance and I hope it is yours.

> *"For God so loved the world, that he gave his only begotten Son, that whosoever believeth in him should not perish, but have everlasting life."*

Returning to Martin Luther, this man is recognized as the "great reformer." As I have studied the Catholic organization and its religion, I cannot find where Luther changed, or reformed, hardly anything within that organization. Because of Luther's protest, he, along with his followers were labeled as "Protestants." Today we have his followers, preachers, and churches founded on and teaching Luther's philosophy as contained in his writings.

It is a misconception to believe that Luther voluntarily left the Catholic Church. He was ***excommunicated.*** He left that organization bringing with him many of its false doctrines; especially two damnable doctrines concerning salvation, that Satan has used to deceive millions into eternal damnation. They are:

1. The doctrine of infant baptism, found nowhere in the Bible.

2. The doctrine of baptismal regeneration. Luther taught that unless you are baptized, you cannot be saved.

When you boil it down, Luther's reformation resulted in churches today named after him, and the projection of the many lies he inherited from the Catholic organization. One would have to conclude since the Catholic organization is still with us, that he was a miserable "reformer." Instead of being a spark to light the Dark Ages, he is the Master Deceiver and Executioner who swings the trap door open to the burning fires of Hell!

Chapter Thirteen

Martin Luther Believed That He and His Preachers Can Forgive Your Sin As God, Himself.

- ***Since Martin Luther agreed with the Roman Catholic organization...***

...that priests could be "mediators between God and man," and could forgive sin, he continued to propagate this false doctrine in his Catechisms. The Pope was able to get Martin Luther out of the Catholic Church; but, no one could get the Catholic Church out of Luther!

Who Can Forgive Sin?
A Minister, Priest, or Jesus Christ?

This question has surfaced numerous times down through the years. One must remember--when you have placed your confidence in any priest or minister as mediator between yourself and God, you have acknowledged them as being equal with Christ. You have then placed yourself in a position to be susceptible to any other false teaching that they present. For any minister or priest to declare that you must go through him to obtain forgiveness of sins is ludicrous, apostate, and diametrically opposed to the Word of God.

Martin Luther, the Master of Deceit, continued this lie by deceiving his followers into thinking that he, himself, and his fellow pastors can forgive your sins. Here are

Luther's own words, as stated in his *Small Catechism*, P.188, under:

"CONFESSION AND ABSOLUTION.

What is Confession? **Confession embraces two parts. One is that we confess our sins; the other, that we received absolution, or forgiveness, from the pastor as from God Himself, and in no wise doubt, but firmly believe, that by it our sins are forgiven before God in Heaven."**

On the same page, under #284, he emphasizes the same,

"...BEFORE THE PASTOR we should confess those sins only which we know and feel in our hearts."

Again on Page 189, he stresses the importance of people obtaining absolution from the Pastor instead of God.

"BEFORE THE PASTOR we should confess *those sins only* which we know and feel in our hearts."

Luther continues this lie to deceive his followers into believing that he and his fellow preachers are replacing God in forgiving your sins. Here are Luther's own words.

> ***"How should we regard the absolution, or forgiveness of sins, pronounced by the Pastor?***
>
> **We should regard the absolution as if pronounced by *God Himself,* and in no wise doubt, but *firmly believe,* that by it *our sins are forgiven before God in Heaven."***

Now that Luther has his followers brainwashed into believing that he and his preachers are standing in God's shoes, with the power to forgive your sins; he continues by instructing the clergy as to what they are to say to the congregation. The Lutheran Pastor, for example, usually instructs the congregation as to what they are to believe and then expects a positive response.

For example: the following is taken and quoted from the writings of the Evangelical Lutheran Synodical Conference of North America and published by the Concordia Publishing House in Saint Louis, Missouri.

1. **The Preacher says:**

> **"Do you promise that with the aid of the Holy Ghost you will henceforth amend your sinful life? Then declare by saying: I do promise."**

2. **The Preacher says:**

> **"Finally, do you believe that THROUGH ME, a called servant of God, you will RECEIVE THE FORGIVENESS OF ALL YOUR SINS? Then declare so by saying: I do believe. As you believe, even so may it be unto you."**

3. **The Preacher says:** (although none of this is found in the Bible), and which is an exact quote from Luther in his *Small Catechism*, P. 190, Par. 287.

THE ABSOLUTION

> **"Upon this your confession, I, BY VIRTUE OF MY OFFICE, AS A CALLED AND ORDAINED SERVANT OF THE LORD, announce the grace of God unto all of you, and in the stead and by the command of my Lord Jesus Christ I FORGIVE YOU ALL YOUR SINS in the name of the Father and of the Son and of the Holy Ghost, Amen."**

To further the heresy that Luther imported from the Catholic Church we find in his *Small Catechism*, Pages 190 and 191, Paragraph 288.

> **"How should we regard the absolution, or forgiveness of sins, pronounced by the pastor?**
>
> **We should regard the absolution as if pronounced by *God Himself* and in no wise**

doubt, but firmly believe, that by it *our sins are forgiven before God in heaven.*

666. Whosesoever sins ye remit, they *are remitted* unto them. *John 20:23.*

667. Whatsoever ye shall loose on earth *shall be loosed in heaven. Matthew 18:18."*

The question many have asked is, "Does the Lutheran preacher forgive his wife's sins also? Does he forgive his children's' sins, and does he forgive HIS OWN SINS?

- ***The Roman Catholic Organization.***

And since similar ideas about Confession and Absolution appear in almost all Catholic literature, the following quotes are from the *Father Connell's Confraternity Edition, New Baltimore Catechism* under "Penance."

1. **"Penance is also a sacrament instituted by Our Divine Savior in which sins committed after Baptism are forgiven through the absolution of the Priest."** (P. 221, Lesson 29, Penance, Question #379).

2. **"The Priest has the power to forgive sins from Jesus Christ, who said to His apostles and to their successors in the Priesthood: 'Receive the Holy Spirit; whose sins you shall forgive, they are forgiven them; whose sins you shall retain, they are**

retained." (John 20:22,23). (P. 221, Lesson 29, Penance, Question #380).

3. **"No man, by his own power and authority, could possibly forgive sins. Only God can do that because sin is an offense against Him. BUT the Priest, as God's representative, can forgive sins because God has given him the power to do so." (Scripture Quotation is Matthew 18:15-18).** (P. 221, Lesson 29, Penance, Question #380, Par. (c)).

4. **"Our Savior could indeed have decreed that men should receive the Pardon of their sins by going directly to God with contrition. BUT a sacrament, administered by men in the name of God, IS A MORE ASSURING AND A MORE EFFECTIVE MEANS."** (P. 223, Lesson 29, Penance, "Important Truths About Penance").

5. **"The power to forgive sins by pronouncing these words of absolution is given to the priest at his ordination. In order to exer-cise this power the priest must have jurisdiction, or be authorized to ACT AS A SPIRITUAL JUDGE OVER THE PERSONS HE ABSOLVES..."** (P. 222, Lesson 29, Penance, Question #381, Par.(a).).

6. **THE PRIEST FORGIVES SINS WITH THE WORDS: 'I absolve thee from thy sins in the name of the Father, and of the Son, and of the Holy Ghost, Amen."** (P. 221, Lesson 29, Penance, Question #381).

One might notice under Point #3 that the Catholic Church acknowledges that no man has the power to forgive sins, but God only. They, then, transfer that power to their priests, who are most certainly only *mortal men*! They give a truth with one hand and take it away with the other hand.

❖ The following Scriptures are those they use to support their position:

1. ***Matthew 9:5-8.***

"For whether is easier, to say, thy sins be forgiven thee; or to say, Arise, and walk? (V.5).

But that ye may know that the Son of man hath power on earth to forgive sins, (then saith he to sick of the palsy,) Arise, take up thy bed, and go into thine house. (V.6).

And he arose and departed to his house. (V.7)

But when the multitudes saw it, they marveled, and glorified God, which had given such power unto men."(V.8).

2. ***Matthew 18:15-18.***

"Moreover if thy brother shall trespass against thee, go and tell him his fault between thee and him alone: if he shall hear thee, thou hast gained thy brother.(V.15).

But if he will not hear thee, then take with thee one or two more, that in the mouth of two or three witnesses every word may be established. (V.16).

And if he shall neglect to hear them, tell it unto the church: but if he neglect to hear the church, let him be unto thee as an heathen man and a publican. (V.17).

"Verily I say unto you, Whatsoever ye shall bind on earth shall be bound in heaven: and whatsoever ye shall loose on earth shall be loosed in heaven." (V.18). (Also used by Martin Luther, *Small Catechism*, Page 182).

3. *John 20:21-23.*

"Then said Jesus to them again, Peace be unto you: as my Father hath sent me, even so send I you. (V.21).

And when he had said this, he breathed on them, and saith unto them; (V.22).

Whose soever sins ye remit, they are remitted unto them; and whosesoever sins ye retain, they are retained." (V.23). (Also used by Martin Luther, *Small Catechism*, Page 183).

4. *Matthew 16:19.*

"And I will give unto thee the keys of the kingdom of heaven: and whatsoever thou shalt bind on earth shall be bound in heaven: and whatsoever thou shalt loose

on earth shall be loosed in heaven." (Also used by Martin Luther, *Small Catechism*, Page 183).

- ***The Purpose of Miracles In The New Testament.***

The 12 Apostles were given power to do healing and miracles; but, ***no*** human being was ever given the power to forgive sin!

We now examine the *purpose of miracles* in the New Testament. Christ performed hundreds of miracles, beginning with His first miracle of turning the water into wine in John 2:1-11. Not all miracles were recorded. John tells us in John 20:30,

> *"And many other signs (Gr. semeion, miracles) truly did Jesus in the presence of his disciples, which are not written in this book."*

The *purpose of the miracles* which *are* recorded, is given in verse 31.

> *"But these are written that ye might believe that Jesus* (His humanity) *is the Christ* (deity, i.e., God in human flesh*), the Son of God* (by the Virgin Birth); *and that believing ye might have life through his name."*

In John 1:11 it is recorded that,

> *"He came unto his own* (Israel) *and his own received him not."*

Christ declared to Israel that He was their Messiah (John 1:41), Savior (Luke 2:11), Sin-bearer (Matthew 1:21), and King (Matthew 2:2); but the religious leaders wanted nothing to do with Him. In Hebrews 2:3, 4 the Word of God declares,

> *"How shall we escape, if we neglect so great salvation; which at the first began to be spoken by the Lord, and was confirmed unto us by them that heard him."*(V.3).
>
> *"God also bearing them* (Israel) *witness, both with SIGNS AND WONDERS, and with DIVERS MIRACLES , and gifts of the Holy Ghost, according to his own will."*(V.4).

In Matthew 9:1-8 Christ had healed a man sick of palsy (a paralytic) as proof that He had the power to forgive sins also. Anyone can say, "I will forgive your sins," but the miracle of healing was "proof positive" that He was truly the Son of God! In Matthew 10:8, this power of healing and other miracles would also be given to the Twelve Apostles, and to The Seventy in Luke 10.

As we are going to see from Scriptures, ***no human being was ever given the power to forgive sins.*** The message of the Twelve Apostles was that Christ was to bear our sin on the cross, and by the power given to them to perform miracles, their message was substantiated as authentic. In Matthew 10:6,7, they were to go ONLY to the nation of Israel.

> *"...go, rather to the lost sheep of the house of Israel. And as ye go, preach, saying, The kingdom of heaven is at hand."* (Matthew 10:6,7).

The power given them is recorded in verse 8...

> *"Heal the sick, cleanse the lepers, raise the dead, cast out devils* (demons): *freely ye have received , freely give."*

Nowhere in Matthew, Chapter 10, do you find they were given power to ***forgive anyone's sins***. Their message and commission was to preach that...

> *...the kingdom of heaven is at hand."*

The reason the Kingdom was "at hand" is that the King was here. When any Jew believed this message, their sins were forgiven. Matthew 1:21 states that,

> *"He* (Christ) *shall save his people from their sins."* (Also note John 1:29).

The Seventy in Luke 10:9,17,19,20 were given the same power to perform miracles. Notice carefully, as you read Luke 10, **NOWHERE do you find the Seventy being given the power to *forgive sins*!** Their message to their own nation was that Jesus Christ was their Savior and Messiah. "Dr. Luke" stated earlier in Luke 2:11,

> *"For unto you is born this day in the city of David a Saviour, which is Christ the Lord."*

Christ's crucifixion and resurrection were God's payment for our sins. Paul declared this in writing to the Ephesians, and we find it in Ephesians 1:7.

> *"In whom we have redemption through his blood, the forgiveness of sins according to the riches of his grace."*

Every minister that loves the Lord Jesus Christ will never draw attention to himself, let alone claim the power to forgive sin. He will declare, as Paul did in I Corinthians 2:2 and I Corinthians 3:1,

> *"For I determined not to know anything among you save Jesus Christ and Him crucified."*

> *" . . .He that glorieth, let him glory in the Lord"* (Not in himself.)"

To the Seventy who preached Christ and him crucified, the Lord said concerning their hearers in Luke 10:16...

> *"He that heareth you heareth me; and he that despiseth you despiseth me; and he that despiseth me despiseth him that sent me."*

Keep in mind, ***it was the message they preached that would be accepted or rejected!*** The message would save or condemn, and that God's word is truth (John 17:17). Ezekiel stated that God's word would be done; i.e., whatever God says He will back it up from Heaven…

> *" . ..but the word which I have spoken shall be done, saith the Lord GOD."* (Ezekiel 12:28).

- ***Scriptural Explanation of "the Keys" and "Binding And Loosing."***

There is no great mystery about this! The same guarantee of God backing up His Word from Heaven, is in Christ's words to Peter in Matthew 16:19…

> *"And I will give unto thee the keys of the kingdom of heaven whatsoever thou shalt bind on earth shall be bound in heaven: and whatsoever thou shalt loose on earth shall be loosed in heaven."*

Vine's Expository Dictionary of Greek New Testament Words has this to say in reference to the Word "bind":

> "The Lord's Words to the Apostle Peter in Matthew 16:19 as to binding, and to all the disciples in 18:18 signify, in the former case, that the apostle, by his ***ministry of the Word of life,*** would keep unbelievers outside the kingdom of God; and admit those who believed."

Thank you, Dr. Vine! It could not be made any clearer! The "keys" are symbolic of the Gospel which, if believed, unlocks Heaven for eternity; or, if rejected, shuts up Heaven to the unbeliever.

The "keys" spoken of in Matthew 16:19 were first used by Peter on the day of Pentecost, as recorded in Acts 2. ***Nowhere did Peter or the Eleven ever even HINT that they could or would forgive anyone's sins!*** The whole chapter is a testimony concerning Christ, the resurrection and His forgiveness. Here are Peter's Words in Acts 2:21,

> *"And it shall come to pass, that whosoever shall call on the name of the Lord shall be saved..*

They were saved because of *the **Word of God*** Peter preached. They were afterwards baptized as a public testimony of their faith. Notice Peter's Words in Acts 2:41…

> *"Then they that gladly <u>received</u> <u>his</u> <u>Word</u> were baptized: and the same day there were added unto them about 3,000 souls."*

Peter used the "keys" (symbolic of God's Word) again in Acts 10. God sent Peter to the Gentile named Cornelius, to show the Jews that the Gentiles could be saved also. Read Chapter 10 and nowhere do you find Peter EVER claimed the power to forgive anyone's sins. Peter directed the lost to Christ and Him alone. Here are Peter's Words in Acts 10:43…

> *"To him* (Christ) *gave all the prophets witness, that through his* (Christ's) *<u>name</u> <u>whosoever</u> <u>believeth</u> <u>in</u> <u>him</u>* (Christ) *<u>shall</u> <u>receive</u> <u>remission</u> <u>of</u> <u>sins</u>."*

Unlike Peter, some clergy, through pride, love to claim this power for themselves and love to mediate between God and man. In doing so they outright deny and resist God' s Word. I Timothy 2:5 blatantly declares that,

> *"For there is one God, and ONE MEDIATOR BETWEEN GOD AND MAN, the man CHRIST JESUS."*

When God's servants preach His Word on earth, it will divide. Those who believe it are saved and, those who do not are lost! It is as simple as that! God's Word is so powerful it will divide as a sharp, two-edged sword (Hebrews 4:12). Isaiah 55:11 declares that His Word will not return unto Him void and empty.

Those in Matthew 16:10 that are bound on earth, are those who have ***believed*** God's WORD and are saved. They have the promises of the Omniscient and Omnipotent God, that in Heaven, He will make good the promises that He gave on earth.

The same goes for those who reject God's Word (John 3:36). Even though many do not believe in Christ, the Word of God, or Hell; it will not alter God's faithfulness to his WORD when he pronounces their sentence in Matthew 25:41…

> *" ...Depart from me ye cursed, into everlasting fire, prepared for the devil and his angels."*

Then they will realize that, not in all the New Testament; nor in Peter's two epistles, was there the vestige, either claimed or exercised, of Peter forgiving anyone's sin.

Who will you believe--man or God? Romans 3:4 makes it perfectly clear concerning God's Word…

> *"God forbid: yea, let God be true, but every man a liar..."*

❖ ***Comparison of John 20:23 to Martin Luther's False Philosophy.***

> *"Whose soever sins ye remit, they are remitted unto them; and whose soever sins ye retain, they are retained."* (John 20:23).

John 20:23 is one of the verses relied upon, as the strongest, to support this position of "binding and loosing" held by Martin Luther and his followers, as well as the Roman Catholic organization. This, they claim, is the right and power given to them by God to forgive your sins.

❖ ***Martin Luther's "Office of the Keys."***

Martin Luther quotes this verse in his *Small Catechism* on Page 181, Part V, giving it the title "The Office of the Keys." Here are his words below:

"What is the Office of the Keys?

> **It is the peculiar church power which Christ has given to His Church on earth to forgive the sins of penitent sinners, but to retain the sins of the impenitent as long as they do not repent."**

By calling this the "Office of the Keys," it reveals a combination of John 20:23 with Matthew 16:19. Martin Luther, to further complete his blasphemy against God's grace, states in his *Small Catechism* on Page 182, Par. 268,

> **268. "Why is this power called the Office of the Keys? This power is called the Office of the Keys because it *opens heaven* by forgiving sins, or *closes heaven* by retaining sins."**

Then, just as the Catholic organization gives a power with one hand and takes it back with another, Martin Luther declares that Christ gave the Church the Office of the Keys. Then the church gives it to the men they ordain as pastors. The evidence is below and the blasphemy is complete!

> ***"How does the local congregation publicly administer the Office of the Keys?*** **According to God's will the Christian congregation chooses and calls men as ministers, who in the name of Christ and in the name of the congregation publicly perform the functions of the Office of the Keys..."**(*Small Catechism*, P. 185, Par. 275.).

> **"The called ministers of Christ preach the Word of God, administer the Sacraments, and through these means of grace offer and convey the forgiveness of sins. This is *as valid,* in heaven also, *as if Christ,* our dear**

> **Lord, *dealt with us Himself.*"** (*Small Catechism*, P.185, 186, Par. 276).

Martin Luther believed that ***he had the power to open or shut heaven*** to poor unfortunate souls!

- ***The Correct Exposition of John 20:23, Or, the Truth of God's Word.***

To obtain the correct teaching of Verse 23, as any Bible student knows, you must compare all other Scriptures that pertain to the same subject or verse in question. When all Scriptures pertaining to the same subject AGREE, you then have the correct teaching of that subject or verse. If not, then you have a wrong interpretation or application of the verse or subject in question. This would then lead to a false teaching perpetrated upon the unsuspecting congregation.

Since all Scripture is given by the "inspiration of God" (II Timothy 3:16), there can be no error or contradiction in God's Word. This is why Peter declared in II Peter 1:20 that...

> *"Knowing this first, that no prophecy of the scripture is of any private interpretation."*

The Word "prophesy" is the Greek "propheteia" and defined by *Vine's Expository Dictionary of Greek New Testament Words:*

> "Signifies the speaking forth of the mind and counsel of God. Though much of the Old

> Testament prophecy was purely predictive, it is the declaration of that which cannot be known by natural means. It is the FORTH-TELLING OF THE WILL OF GOD, WHETHER WITH REFERENCE TO THE PAST, THE PRESENT, OR THE FUTURE."

This does not mean that one cannot understand the Scriptures for themselves. It does warn against anyone building a doctrine on one, *isolated,* verse without comparing all other verses on the same subject.

As we have learned from previous chapters, Martin Luther, the Master of Deceit, has no problem with taking Scripture out of context, removing words, or adding words. This is *why* the Holy Spirit inspired Paul in his second epistle to Timothy, 2:15, to emphasize the value of studying the Word of God for yourself.

> *"Study to shew thyself approved unto God, a workman that needeth not to be ashamed, rightly dividing the Word of truth."*

Rightly dividing comes from the Greek Word "orthotom" and means *"teaching Scripture accurately"*. Our study thus far has shown that only God, Who is Christ in human flesh, can forgive sins.

Now let us compare John 20:23 with some other Scriptures concerning forgiveness of sins, and a preacher or priest trying to place himself as mediator and intercessor between God and man..

A mediator is one who goes between God and man. There have been and still are myriads of men, either claiming they are the Christ, or that they possess special powers above others in order to be man's representative to God. Maybe you are one who actually believes your minister or priest can forgive your sins; thereby instilling in you the confidence that you are now ready for eternity. Let us examine the BIBLE and see if you have been misled, or if their claims are substantiated. Here is God's Word on the subject:

1. ***I Timothy* 2:5.** *"For there is one God, and one mediator between God and men, the man Christ Jesus;"*

2. **Romans 8:34.** *"Who is he that condemneth? It is Christ that died, yea rather, that is risen again, who is even at the right hand of God, who also maketh intercession for us."*

3. **John 14:6.** *"Jesus saith unto him, I am the way, the truth, and the life: no man cometh unto the Father, but by me."*

4. **Hebrews 7:25.** *"Wherefore he* (Christ) *is able also to save them to the uttermost that come unto God by him (* *Christ), seeing He* (Christ) *ever liveth to make intercession for them."*

5. **Isaiah 53:12** *".. .and he* (Christ) *bare the sin of many, and made intercession for the transgressors."*

6. **Hebrews 7:25.** *"Wherefore he* (Christ) *is able also to save them to the uttermost that come unto God by him*

(Christ), *seeing He* (*Christ*) *ever liveth to make intercession for them."*

7. ***I John 2:1.*** *"My little children,. these things write I unto you, that ye sin not. And if any man sin, we have an advocate with the Father, Jesus Christ the righteous."*

8. ***Isaiah 53:12.*** *".. .and he* (Christ) *bare the sin of many, and made intercession for the transgressors."*

One would have to outright deny the Word of God and call Jesus Christ a liar by not acknowledging that Christ, and He alone, is the only One who can forgive our sins. Isaiah 53:5,6 describes the lost condition of man and what our wonderful Savior did for us. No wonder He is a jealous God!

> *"But he* (Christ) *was wounded for our transgressions, he* (Christ) *was bruised for our iniquities: the chastisement of our peace was upon him* (Christ): *and with his stripes we are healed."*(V.5).
>
> *"All we like sheep have gone astray; we have turned every one to his own way and the LORD hath laid on him* (Christ) *the iniquity of us all."* (V.6).

- ***The only One who can forgive sins is the One who paid for our sins, and that is Jesus Christ.***

The only true and absolute peace a person can possess concerning eternal life comes from Jesus Christ and

His payment for sin. Paul makes this perfectly clear in Romans 5:1…

> *"Therefore being justified by faith, we have peace with God through our Lord Jesus Christ."*

Scriptures are vouchsafed in plenty for those who have a sincere desire to know the truth. Tradition has propagated upon humanity the most dastardly evil employed by Martin Luther and his followers, as well as other clergy, to convince the unsuspecting that they have the power of Jesus Christ to forgive your sins.

The following Scriptures will unmask the veil of error and illuminate the truth of God's Word:

1. ***Mark 2:10***. *"But that ye may know that the Son of Man* (Christ) *hath power on earth to forgive sins."*

2. ***Luke 5:20.*** *"And when he* (Christ) *saw their faith, he* (Christ) *said unto him, Man, thy sins are forgiven thee."*

3. ***Matthew 9:6.*** *"But that ye may know that the Son of man* (Christ) *hath power on earth to forgive sins,..."*

4. ***Ephesians 4:32.****"And be ye kind one to another, tenderhearted, forgiving one another, even as God for Christ's sake hath forgiven you."*

5. **Colossians 2:13.** *"And you, being dead in your sins and the uncircumcision of your flesh, hath he*

quickened together with him (Christ), *having forgiven you ALL TRESPASSES."*

6. ***I Corinthians 15:3.*** *"For I delivered unto you first of all that which I also received, how that Christ died for our sins according to the scriptures."*

7. ***I Peter 3:18.*** *"For Christ also hath once suffered for sins, the just for the unjust, that he* (Christ) *might bring us to God, being put to death in the flesh, but quickened by the Spirit."*

8. ***John 1:29.*** *"The next day John seeth Jesus coming unto him, and saith, Behold the Lamb of God, which taketh away the sin of the world. "* (I don't see anything in this verse that indicates the priest or minister is the one who takes away sin.).

9. ***Romans 11:27.*** *"For this is my covenant unto them, When I* (Christ) *shall take away their sins."*

10. **Acts 13:38.** *Be it known unto you, therefore, men and brethren, that through this man* (Christ) *is preached unto you the forgiveness of sins."*

This is what every Lutheran minister and Catholic priest should be preaching; ie., that *through Jesus Christ*, and Him alone, is the forgiveness of sin.

Our question is, and should be yours also, why are they not directing their parishioners to Christ instead of themselves? I, personally, have asked hundreds of people belonging to these two organizations to question their minister or priest, asking them why they cannot just go directly to Jesus Christ for forgiveness? Most often their answer is, "I wouldn't dare do something like that." My reply, "Why not, are you scared to?

You have a right to question your pastor or priest on ANYTHING they teach." I *certainly* get questioned, and it doesn't bother me as the Word of God backs me up every time!

Sad to say, the Lutheran clergy, being trained in "Luther's" seminaries, following Luther's philosophy, have almost promoted themselves to the level of a god in the eyes of their people, a practice so entrenched that their congregations feel it would be a "sin" to question their authority! It is obvious that the same is true of the Roman Catholic organization. Sad to say, that organization is able to hide the grossest of sin and are arrogant enough to be *insulted* when questioned about it.

We find the prophet, Jeremiah, experienced the same problem, so nothing has changed in over 2500 years*!*

> *"The prophets prophesy falsely, and the priests bear rule by their means; and my people love to have it so: and what will ye do in the end thereof?"* (Jeremiah 5:31).

11. ***Acts 13:39.*** *"And by him* (Christ) *all that believe are justified* (declared *righteous) from all things, from which ye could not be justified by the law of Moses."*

(Please note: By believing...in Jesus Christ we are justified.)

12. ***Ephesians* 1:7.** *"In whom we have redemption through his (Christ's) blood, the forgiveness of sins, according to the riches of his grace."*

Remember--***nowhere*** in the New Testament can you find ***one*** case where any of the Apostle's ever forgave anyone's sin. They always pointed their listeners to Jesus Christ. If not one of the Apostles ever made that claim, then those today claiming that power have placed themselves above the Apostles, and equal with Jesus Christ, Himself.

❖ ***Luke 7:47,48,50.***

"Wherefore I (Christ) *say unto thee, Her sins, which are many, are forgiven..."*

In verse 48, Christ assures this woman her sins have been forgiven:

"And He (Christ) *said unto her, Thy sins are forgiven."*

In verse 50 the Lord gives the *reason* the woman's sins were forgiven. It is on the same basis that our sins are forgiven--our FAITH IN HIM--and not in a minister or priest. No priest or minister ever died for your sins, but Christ did.

"And he (Christ) *said to the woman, Thy faith hath saved thee; go in peace."*

The Lord Jesus Christ forgave sins while he was on the earth, and is still the ***only One*** who can forgive sins today. Every preacher and priest is a sinner themselves, and needs forgiveness. Notice God's indictment on mankind in Romans 3:23…

> *"For all have sinned and come short of the glory of God."*

My Bible says *"ALL have sinned"*; and I cannot find where it says, "ALL, but preachers and priests." *"Coming short of the glory of God"* literally means "falling short of being as righteous as God, Himself." Therefore, Romans 3:24, 25 tell us how and why we have remission of sins.

> *"Being justified freely by his grace through the redemption that is in Christ Jesus: Whom God hath set forth to be a propitiation through faith in his* (Christ's) *blood, to declare his righteousness far the remission of sins that are past, through the forbearance of God."* (Romans 3:24,25).

Where do you find anything about a minister or priest being able to remit your sins? Ask your minister or priest if they are trusting Jesus Christ as the payment for *their* sin. The clergy go to Heaven the same way the congregation does, that is through Christ and Him alone. If their answer is "Yes," then ask them why you cannot go directly to Christ the same as they?

The only One who can forgive sin is the One who is sinless. In II Corinthians 5:17 the Bible declares that Christ was without sin.

"For he hath made him (Christ) *to be sin* (i.e. the payment for sin) *for us, who knew no sin; that we might be made the righteousness of God in him."*

- ***Would any minister or priest dare to claim they are sinless?***

Remember--only the One who is without sin can forgive those who are sinners, and that is Christ Jesus. By making the claim they can forgive sins, they are actually placing themselves on equality with Christ and being sinless themselves.

I, personally, have talked to many and all deny they are sinless, but still become quite offended that one should question their self-appointed authority. Even though they deny this, their solicitation for sinners to come to them for forgiveness is an indictment against themselves by their own WORD AND PRACTICE..

❖ ***I John 1:8-10.***

"If we say that we have no sin, we deceive ourselves, and the truth is not in us." (V.8).

"If we confess our sins, he (Christ) *is faithful and just to forgive us our sins, and to cleanse us from all unrighteousness."* (V.9).

"If we say that we have not sinned, we make him a liar, and his (Christ's) *Word is not in us."* (V.10).

The First Chapter of I John is written to Christians who sin AFTER they are saved. John is addressing the Christian's service, not salvation. His fellowship with Christ, and not his Sonship. His power for Christ as a witness, not his position with Christ in Heaven. Let us closely analyze what I John 1:8-10 actually says.

1. Who are we to confess our sins to?
   Answer: Jesus Christ.

2. Who is faithful to forgive our sins?
   Answer: Jesus Christ.

3. Who is able to cleanse us from all unrighteousness?
   Answer: Jesus Christ.

Should any Lutheran minister who follows Martin Luther, or a priest, even hint that they, themselves, are without sin, God says they are SELF DECEIVED (I John 1:8), and make God a liar (I John 1:10) .

I have been a pastor for 36 years and it is beyond my comprehension to even think I could forgive someone's sins so they could *be saved*; or, think they are *keeping themselves saved*! Of course, I forgive those who have offended me; but, that is something different altogether. That is just a personal thing and has nothing to do with where a person spends eternity.

What a blessing it has been, and still is, to direct people to our Wonderful Savior, who will forgive any and all sins. John 6:37 declares,

> *" and him that cometh to me* (Christ) *I will in no wise cast out."*

There are multitudes of Scriptures in addition to what we have already quoted. Isaiah 43:25; 44:22; 53:5,6; Micah 7:18; Exodus 34:7; Daniel 9:17-19; and Psalm 130:1-4, could have been quoted, as well as many others.

- ***Faithful Ministry of the Gospel Gives Remittance of Sin!***

What follows is an examination of the verse most commonly used by Lutheran ministers and Catholic priests to justify their "power" in claiming they can forgive your sins. By this, they place themselves as the mediator between you and God.

> *"Whose soever sins ye remit they are remitted unto them; and whose soever sins ye retain, they are retained."* (John 20:23).

As we compare other verses with John 20:23, we can easily see the only way a Christian, clergy, or layman, can remit sins is by presenting the WORD OF GOD. The Word will judge those who reject it, as Christ stated in John 12:48,

> *"He that rejecteth me* (Christ), *and receiveth not my Words , hath one that judgeth him: the WORD that I have spoken, the same* (i.e., the Word) *shall judge him in the last day."*

In Psalm 138:2 God relates how important the Word of God is:

> *"I will . . . praise thy name for thy lovingkindness and for thy truth: FOR THOU HAST MAGNIFIED THY WORD ABOVE ALL THY NAME."*

The reason the WORD is magnified above His name is that we today would not know the surety of God or His name, if it were not for the WORD OF GOD.

When a Christian witnesses to a lost person with the WORD of God, as recorded in John 3:16 and 36, that person then has a choice to make. If they accept Christ, they have everlasting life. Should they reject Christ until death, they will then experience the wrath of God in Hell, just as the Word of God has stated in John 3:36…

> *"He that believeth on the Son hath ever-lasting life: and he that believeth not the Son shall not see life; but the WRATH OF GOD abideth on him."*

When one believes God' s WORD, their sins are then ***remitted***, not by the preacher or priest; but by the WORD OF GOD which promises them eternal life.

Should they ***reject*** God's WORD, they will ***retain*** their sin. Only by presenting God's Word as a faithful witness for Christ, do we have a part in another person's salvation. This is what Christ meant in John 20:23 when he told His disciples that...

> *"Whose soever sins ye remit, they are remitted unto them, and whose soever sins ye retain they are retained."*

The Greek Word for "remit" is "*aphiemi*" and literally means "to send away." *Vine's Expository Words in the Greek New Testament* explains the use of this verb as such.

> "Scripture makes clear that the Lord's Words could not have been intended to bestow the exercise of absolution which the Scripture declares is the prerogative of God alone. There is no instance in the New Testament of this act on the part of the Apostles. The Words are to be understood in a "declarative" sense; the statement has regard to the effects of their ministry of the gospel, with its two-fold effects of remission or retention."

- ***None of the Apostles Ever Claimed the Power to Forgive Sins.***

  - Search the New Testament through and you will not find where any of the Apostles ever claimed the power or authority to forgive anyone's sins. The Apostles always directed the lost to Christ, and Him alone, as the One who paid for sin and offers forgiveness to all in return for their faith.

  - ***Fact***: The minister or priest who asks you to trust him as God's representative to forgive your sin has placed himself as mediator between you and God. God's Word in I Timothy 2:5 states, with no uncertainty,

> *"For there is one God, and one mediator between God and men, the man Christ Jesus."*

If you are one who is trusting one of Luther's preachers or the Catholic priest to forgive your sins, instead of Jesus Christ, you will spend eternity separated from God. Christ encountered these same types of religious leaders in His day and levied a stern rebuke against them. Consider Matthew 23:13…

> *"But unto you, scribes and Pharisees, Hypocrites! for ye shut up the kingdom of heaven against men: for ye neither go in yourselves, neither suffer ye them that are entering to go in."*

An analysis of this verse will show the strength of Christ's Words against these RELIGIOUS LEADERS:

- ***The Scribes.*** In New Testament times the Scribes were the students, interpreters, and teachers of the Old Testament Scriptures, and were held in high esteem by the people. They were also called lawyers in Matthew 22:35. They were avowed opponents of Christ, and were publicly denounced by Him for making the Word of God of none effect through their tradition.

- ***Pharisees.*** The name means" separated" and they were called" separatists" because they had separated themselves from the ambitious political party in their nation. They were the exponents and guardians of the written and oral law, and, in belief, were the "conservatives" in distinction from the Sadducees. Their religious orthodoxy was spiritually dead and barren. These were the religious leaders--just as you have today!

❖ ***"Hypocrites!"*** Christ called the Scribes and Pharisees "Hypocrites" because they were aware that what they were teaching the people was not true. Christ knew this and that is why He labeled them correctly. Your minister may appear to be very humble and sincere on the surface, but when he tells you that he can forgive your sins, his true character is then exposed. Christ has this to say in Matthew 23:27…

> *" . . . for ye are like unto whited sepulchres which indeed appear beautiful outward, BUT are within full of dead men's bones, and of all uncleanness."*

If you believe the false teaching of today's modern" scribes and pharisees", you will not enter the Kingdom of Heaven. *"For ye shut up the Kingdom of Heaven against men."* I will be more specific. I am referring to the followers of Martin Luther and the Roman Catholic organization.

These false teachers are not saved and will not enter the Kingdom of Heaven, but Hell awaits their entry. *"For ye neither go in yourselves."*

Who do these ministers and priests confess their sins to? Do they forgive themselves? Have you ever heard one of these clergymen telling their congregation who they confess their sin to? If you support these churches with your money, you surely have a right to know how the Lutheran ministers or Catholic priests get their sins forgiven. Why not ask them?

Have they presented themselves to you as being without sin? I should hope not, but if that is the case with some, then, according to I John 1:8, God would indict them with "First Degree LYING".

> *"If we say we have no sin, we deceive ourselves* (not others)*, and the truth is not in us."*

In Luke 23:43, it was Jesus Christ who forgave the thief on the cross next to Him. He didn't call for the religious leaders or the priests, did He? Only Christ could assure this thief that his sins were forgiven and give Him the absolute assurance that *"TODAY SHALT THOU BE WITH ME IN PARADISE."*

Who are you going to trust for your salvation, the Lutheran minister who follows the writings of a man dead some 460 years ago, the Catholic priest, or JESUS CHRIST?

Ask the ministers and priests who assume the power to forgive your sins by claiming Matthew 9:8, why do they not claim and practice the power God gave the Apostles in Matthew 10:8?

"Heal the sick, cleanse the leper, raise the dead, cast out devils (demons)*: freely ye have received, freely give."*

As Christ stated in Matthew 9: 5…

"For whether is easier, to say, Thy sins be forgiven thee; or to say, Arise and walk?"

If these Lutheran ministers and Catholic priests can legitimately forgive your sins, let us see proof of their claims such as: healing the sick, cleansing the lepers, or RAISING THE DEAD!

Notice the paradox. The Apostles had, and exercised, the powers given them by Christ in Matthew 10:8; but, NEVER claimed to possess the power to *forgive anyone's sin.*

The Lutheran and Catholic clergy claim the power to forgive your sins; yet, are unable to exercise the power to heal the sick, raise the dead, etc. If they possess the power the Apostles had, let us take them to the nearest hospital and let us witness the healing of every person in that hospital. If they fail, you have exposed a false teacher who pretends to be humble, pious, a lover of God and etc. This all seems so convincing until compared with the Word of God.

Again, may I submit, IT IS MUCH EASIER TO SAY TO SOMEONE, *"I forgive your sins"* than to say *"Arise and walk."* Put them to the test and you will find their claims and teaching to be fraudulent.

Whether in the secular or ecclesiastical arena, men have always craved to have power over others. Martin Luther, the Master of Deceit, continues to convince men today that they *have* that power. Christ indicted the religious leaders for their pride.

Here are Christ's Words in Matthew 23:5, 6, 28,

> *"But all their works they do for to be seen of men: they make broad their phylacteries, and enlarge the borders their garments,"* (V.5).

> *"And love the uppermost rooms at feasts, and the chief seats in the synagogues."* (V.6).

> *"Even so ye also outwardly appear righteous unto men, but within ye are full of hypocrisy and iniquity."* (V.8).

Conclusion: There is only one Person who can forgive your sin. There is only one Person who paid for your sin. There is only one Person who is your Mediator, and there is only one Person who can give you eternal life. That Person is the LORD JESUS CHRIST.

Whether you go to Heaven or Hell depends on who you want to believe, Martin Luther, his puppet preachers, the Catholic priest, or THE LORD JESUS CHRIST!

> *"Jesus saith unto him* (or you), *I am the way, the truth, and the life: no man cometh unto the Father, but by me."* (John14:6).

Personally, if I were visiting a church where the preacher got up and stated he would forgive my sins, I would get up and walk out immediately. I would not subject myself or my family to that type of brainwashing; but would find myself a good, Bible-teaching church where Jesus Christ is exalted, not the preacher!

The Lord Jesus Christ died on a cruel, Roman cross to pay the sin debt of mankind. Three days and nights later, He was resurrected showing God had accepted His payment for sin. If you will believe that Jesus Christ died for you, personally, He will give you the righteousness you need to go to Heaven. The price is paid. Will you reach out and accept it by faith?

> *"For he hath made him to be sin for us, who knew no sin; that we might be made the righteousness of God in him."* (II Corinthians 5:21).

Our prayer is that you *will* accept the Lord Jesus Christ as your personal Savior, and *have* the peace and assurance of eternal life in Heaven when this life is through. Jesus Christ, *only*, can forgive sin!

> *"These things have I written unto you that believe on the name of the Son of God; that ye may know that ye have eternal life, and that ye may believe on the name of the Son of God."* (I John 5:13).

Chapter Fourteen

An Open Letter From The Author

Dear Friend:

After reading this book, may I address you with a very simple and personal question? If you were to die tonight, do you know absolutely, without a single doubt that you will go to Heaven when you leave this earth? The only way any person can have this assurance and peace is by trusting the Word of God to be true. I hope that you do.

1. ***There is only one way to Heaven. Christ said in John 14:6,***

> *"Jesus saith unto him, I am the way, the truth, and the life: no man cometh unto the Father, but by me* (Christ)." (John 14:6).

2. ***There is only one payment for sin, as recorded in John 3:16,***

> *"For God so loved the world, that he gave his only begotten Son* (Jesus Christ), *that whosoever believeth in him should not perish, but have everlasting life."* (John 3:16).

Jesus Christ suffered and gave His life on the cross as payment for the sin of every human being ever born. He wants you and I to live in Heaven with Him for all eternity. Since we all have sinned (Romans 3:23) and the payment for sin is death (Romans 6:23), we have a big problem! There will be no sin in Heaven.

3. *There are two choices.*

You can pay for your own sin in Hell, i.e., the Lake of Fire; or, accept the payment Christ made for you on the cross. His suffering and death on the cross paid the price for all sin. His resurrection showed the payment was accepted by God. We accept His payment for our sin and He gives us the righteousness we need for Heaven. Salvation, eternal life, however you want to say it, is a gift our Lord paid for by His death on the cross.

> *"For he hath made him to be sin for us, who knew no sin; that we might be made the righteousness of God in him."* (II Corinthians 5:21).

4. *There is only one kind of faith.*

God will never accept your faith in your own good works. Things like baptism, confirmation, social standing, giving financially to the church, church membership; or, any works of the flesh will never merit you eternal life. It would be an insult to God, since He allowed His Son to make the ultimate sacrifice for all mankind, for you to think you have something better to offer. Salvation is only received as a gift from God.

> *"For by grace are ye saved through faith; and that not of yourselves: it is the gift of God: Not of works, lest any man should boast."* (Ephesians 2:8-9).

5. *Your absolute assurance from God's Word.*

> *"He that believeth on the Son hath everlasting life: and he that believeth not the Son shall not see life; but the wrath of God abideth on him."* (John 3:36).
>
> *"These things have I written unto you that believe on the name of the Son of God; that ye may know that ye have eternal life, and that ye may believe on the name of the Son of God."* (I John 5:13).

If reading this book has helped you in any way to trust Jesus Christ, and Him alone, for your salvation, please write or email and allow me to rejoice with you.

I pray that you will reach out by faith and receive the gift of eternal life right now, before it is too late.

Sincerely,

Dr. Max D. Younce
P.O. Box 573
Walnut Grove, MN 56180
www.heritagebbc.com

BIBLIOGRAPHY

Strong's Exhaustive Concordance Of The Bible
James Strong, S.T.D., LL.D
Abingdon Press, New York, Nashville

Vine's Expository Dictionary of New Testament Words
W.E. Vine, M.A.
Hendrickson Publishers, Peabody, Massachusetts

The Book of Concord – translated and edited by Theodore G. Tappert, Jaroslav Pelikan, Robert H. Fischer, Arthur C. Piepkorn (Collaborators).
Fortress Press, Philadelphia, Pennsylvania

The *Large Catechism* of Martin Luther
Translated by Robert H. Fischer
Fortress Press, Philadelphia, Pennsylvania

Luther's Small Catechism
Concordia Publishing House, St. Louis, Missouri

"Filled With The Spirit, The Book of Acts, A Verse-by-Verse Commentary
John R. Rice, D.D., Litt.D.
Sword of the Lord Publishers
Murfreesboro, Tennessee

"Baptized: Marked For Living!
John D. Hopper, Min.D.
Sacred Heart, Minnesota

The Bible, God's Written Word
King James Translation

History of the Christian Church
Philip Schaaf

Martin Luther, General Teachings/Activities
Biblical Discernment Ministries
www.rapidnet.com/~jbeard/bdm/luther/general.htm.

Martin Luther's Sacramental Gospel
Biblical Discernment Ministries
www.rapidnet.com~jbeard/exposes/luther.general.htm

Martin Luther's Preface to the Small Catechism
www.edccs.com/redeemer/beliefs/smallcatechism.htm

www.worldfuturefund.org

Medieval Sourcebook: Martin Luther (1483-1546)
The Jews and their Lies, Excerpts (1543).

Note: I could have filled *pages* with Bibliography references and documentation from *thousands* who denounce Luther' lies and his false religion of salvation by baptism; instead of faith in the death and resurrection of Jesus Christ alone for salvation. This book is between Luther's false philosophy and the Word of God; therefore, the Bibliography is kept a minimum.

Scripture Index

Acts

Romans

Revelation Continued

AUTHOR BIOGRAPHY

Dr. Younce has been in the ministry 37 years, having been ordained in 1970. In his latest book, *Martin Luther, Master of Deceit*, he has written a classic, exposing the doctrinal heresies taught by Martin Luther. It is written in a scholarly manner; but, easy to read and comprehend by the average layman.

The book is well documented by quoting Martin Luther from his own Catechisms; so, there is no mistake as to what this man believed!

You will reap a wealth of information concerning Luther's philosophy of baptismal regeneration, i.e., you receive eternal life when you are baptized. This is a false doctrine diametrically opposed to God's Word.

Luther and his "puppet preachers" have led, and still are leading millions into eternal hell by teaching them to trust in their water baptism, instead of the death and resurrection of Jesus Christ, and Him ***alone*** for their salvation.

Other books by Dr. Younce include: *A Biblical Examination of Hell*, (several diagrams are included); *A Biblical Examination of Baptism; Not Chosen To Salvation,*(refuting the false doctrine of predestination for salvation); *Who Can Forgive Sins? A Minister, Priest, Or Jesus Christ?*; *Face To Face With Tongues*; *Salvation And The Public Invitation; The Truth About Evolution, Or, Don't Let Satan Make A Monkey Out of You!*

PROPERTY
CHRISTIAN BIBLE